WOOD FINISHER'S HANDBOOK

WOOD FINISHER'S HANDBOOK

Sam Allen

Sterling Publishing Co. Inc. New York

Library of Congress Cataloging in Publication Data

Allen, Sam.
   Wood finisher's handbook.

   Includes index.
   1. Wood finishing.   I. Title.
TT325.A45   1984   684'.084   84-8522
ISBN 0-8069-7914-3 (pbk.)

      9   10

Copyright © 1984 by Sterling Publishing Co., Inc.
Two Park Avenue, New York, N.Y. 10016
Distributed in Canada by Oak Tree Press Ltd.
℅ Canadian Manda Group, P.O. Box 920, Station U
Toronto, Ontario, Canada M8Z 5P9
Distributed in Great Britain and Europe by Cassell PLC
Artillery House, Artillery Row, London SW1P 1RT, England
Distributed in Australia by Capricorn Ltd.
P.O. Box 665, Lane Cove, NSW 2066
Manufactured in the United States of America

ACKNOWLEDGMENTS

The material in this book is based largely on the experience I have gained during my career as a woodworker so I would like to acknowledge those that have helped me gain that experience.

My wife, Virginia, who is an accomplished woodworker in her own right, has helped me with many projects. Without her help in preparing the manuscript this book would not have been possible. My brother, John Allen, helped with many of the photos. His hands appear throughout the book.

I would like to thank my mother, Betty Allen. Her encouragement early in my life enabled me to pursue a career in woodworking and she helped in preparing this book. Her knowledge of chemistry was a valuable resource in preparing the chemical stain section.

Marcella and Mel Van Orman gave me my first set of tools when I was a boy, and I appreciate their encouragement.

Roger Roylance, who has been my friend since grade school, worked with me on some of my first projects; we developed our skills together. He has always encouraged me to strive for better quality work.

I would like to thank all of the dedicated shop teachers that helped to instill a love for wood in me. The instructors and professors in the woodworking department at Brigham Young University, where I received my formal training, are very knowledgeable and I appreciate the instruction I received from them.

I am particularly grateful to the foremen and crews that I have worked with for sharing the knowledge they have gained over the years.

Most of the photos in this book were taken by the author, Sam Allen. Additional photos were supplied by Minwax Co. Inc.; Bassett Furniture Industries, Inc.; Parks Woodworking Machine Co.; Shopsmiths, Inc.; 3M Industrial Abrasives Division; Great Neck Saw Mfrs., Inc.; Garrett Wade Co., Inc.; Norton; General Wood Works Co., Inc.; DeVilbiss; Watvo-Dennis Corp.; P & P Chair Co.; Fancher Furniture Co., Inc.; Hyde Manufacturing Co./The Old-House Journal; Master Appliance Corp./The Old-House Journal; Fine Hardwoods/American Walnut Assn.; American Technical Publishers, Inc., "Woodworking: Tools, Materials, Processes" by William P. Spence and L. Duane Griffiths, © 1981.

Contents

Introduction

Wood finishing is an art as well as a craft. Before you can practice the art of creative wood finishing, you must become proficient at the craft of wood finishing. There are many basic skills to be mastered before you can consider yourself an expert wood finisher, but along the way to becoming an expert you can produce many beautifully finished pieces. Some finishes can be effectively applied even by the most inexperienced beginner.

Modern techniques and equipment not only make it easier than ever for the beginner to achieve good results; they allow the advanced finisher more freedom to exercise creativity in finishing.

The first section of this book covers the basics of wood finishing from wood preparation through the finish coat. If you have never applied a wood finish before, this section will lead you step by step through the entire finishing process. Those of you who already have experience finishing will still find the first section useful because it includes some of the most up-to-date techniques, along with traditional methods that still provide results other methods don't. For example, the chapter on wood preparation covers the newest form of wood surfacing, abrasive planing, as well as one of the older forms of smoothing wood, scraping.

The second section of the book covers advanced techniques that give the experienced finisher more options and creative control over the finishing process. Topics covered in this section include mixing your own stains, chemical stains and wood graining, along with many others. Once you have mastered the basics covered in the first section, the topics discussed in the second section will open up new areas for you to explore. Many of the processes discussed in the second section are traditional techniques that have been largely forgotten during the past few years because of the easy-to-use new finishes, but some of the effects created by these traditional methods are hard to duplicate by any other means. For example, chemical stains color the wood without obscuring any of the natural beauty of the wood. They actually change the chemical composition of the wood, altering its color without covering the surface with a coating of pigment.

ABOUT WOOD

Wood is a complex material with a wide range of characteristics. To fully take advantage of the finishing process, you need to understand a little about the character and unique properties of the wood you are working with.

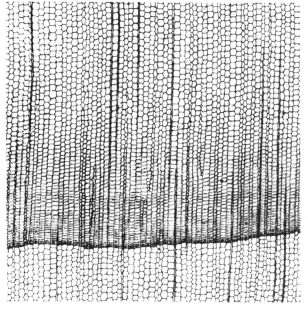

Illus. 1. A cross section of western red cedar, greatly enlarged.

Wood is composed of elongated cells that vary in length from ⅛ in. to 1/25 in. depending on the species of wood. In a living tree these cells are filled with fluids. When a tree is cut and dried for lumber the cells dry out and become hollow. The cells are connected to each other by a natural glue called lignin. Wood's fibrous properties are a result of these long cells that are all connected by lignin. (Illus. 1)

A tree grows by forming new cells in a layer just below the bark called the cambium. The grain pattern that gives wood its desirable ornamentation is formed in the cambium as the cells are formed. Periods of rapid growth in the spring create cells that are large and less dense, while the slower growth of summer produces cells that are smaller and more dense. Together the spring growth and the summer growth produce an annual ring. One ring is formed for each year of the tree's life. When a log is cut into lumber many annual rings are cut through. The grain pattern is formed by the angle at which the saw cuts through the cells that make up the ring.

There are three general ways that lumber can be cut and each produces a different type of grain. Plain sawing is the most economical way to cut solid lumber, so it is the most prevalent. Plain-sawed lumber is cut so that the saw blade passes almost tangent to the annual rings. The grain produced is called a flat grain and is the familiar series of long arcs or parabolas.

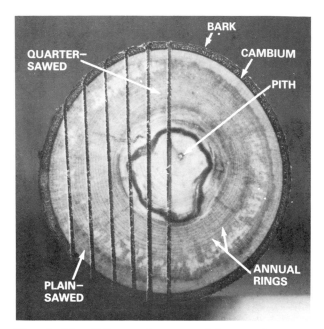

Illus. 2. The difference between plain-sawed lumber and quarter-sawed lumber is a result of how the blade intersects the annual rings. In plain-sawed lumber the saw blade cuts through the rings at an angle of 45 degrees or less. The angle between the blade and the rings approaches 90 degrees in quarter-sawed lumber.

Quarter-sawed lumber is cut so that the saw blade passes at about a 90 degree angle to the annual rings. The grain produced is called a vertical or edge grain. It is characterized by a long parallel grain pattern.

If a log is placed in a stationary position for cutting and left in that position throughout the cutting process, both plain sawed and quarter-sawed lumber will be produced. As the first cuts are made, the blade will be tangent to the annual rings producing plain sawed lumber; as the cutting proceeds through the log, the angle of the annual rings in relation to the blade will become closer to 90 degrees as the blade moves towards the center of the log, producing quarter-sawed lumber. After passing the center and moving towards the other side of the log, the boards will again be plain-sawed. (Illus. 2). It is possible to maximize the production of either plain-sawed or quarter-sawed lumber by repositioning the log during the sawing.

The third way of cutting lumber is used only for producing veneer or plywood. It is called rotary cutting. In this method the log is placed in a giant lathe and rotated; a knife blade peels a thin slice of wood from the surface of the log. The cutting all takes place parallel to the annual rings. This produces a very widely spaced grain pattern because the knife only cuts across the annual rings at a very shallow angle as it spirals in to the center of the log. Some species of wood exhibit a very wild grain pattern when they are cut by the rotary method. The familiar wild grain of fir plywood is a good example. However, not all woods exhibit this wild grain when rotary cut. Birch plywood is almost always rotary cut and the grain produced is pleasing. Rotary-cut oak is frequently used for doors or plywood and its grain is not objectionably wild. The major advantage of rotary cutting is that long wide pieces of veneer are produced. A sheet of plywood can be made without any joints in the face veneer when rotary cut veneer is used.

Veneers can also be flat sliced, which is the equivalent of plain sawing, or it can be quarter sliced. Both of these methods produce veneer of varying widths depending on the diameter of the log it was sliced from. The piece of log that the veneer is cut from is called a flitch. Veneer cut from the same flitch will match closely, especially if the veneer is used in the same sequence as it was cut.

In the growing tree, fluids must be transported from the roots to other areas of the tree. To accomplish this, many small channels or pores are formed in the wood. In some species, such as oak, the pores are large. Wood in this category is called open grained because the surface of a board cut from this type of tree will have a distinct texture created by these pores. Other species like birch have pores that are much smaller and less noticeable. This type is called a closed grain wood.

Another type of fluid channel is called a medullary ray cell. It is a long passageway that radiates out from the center of the tree to the edges. In some woods it is very pronounced and forms a prominent grain feature. Oak is a prime example of a wood that exhibits prominent rays. In plain-sawed oak the rays appear as small dark lines running parallel with the grain, but when the wood is quarter sawed the rays show up as large irregularly shaped markings that run across the grain. (Illus. 3). Quarter-sawed oak that has a lot of ray marks is sometimes called tiger oak.

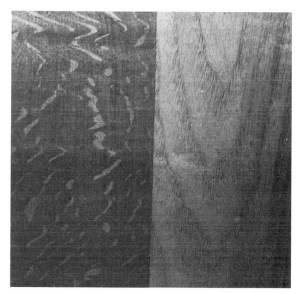

Illus. 3. The quarter-sawed English oak on the left exhibits prominent ray marks. The plain-sawed persimmon on the right shows the characteristic parabolic grain pattern of plain-sawed wood.

At the center of the tree is a small-diameter area of soft, usually dark-colored wood called pith. This is the wood that was first formed when the tree was a sapling. Surrounding the pith is the heartwood. This area makes up most of the diameter of the tree. The heartwood is essentially dead. The sapwood surrounds the heartwood; it is composed of the most recent annual rings of the tree. In some trees there is a variation in color between the sapwood and the heartwood. For example, the heartwood of the walnut tree is dark brown while the sapwood is a light cream color.

Knots are formed where a branch connects to the main trunk of the tree. The annual rings are displaced around a knot creating a variation in the grain. In plain-sawed lumber knots usually appear round or oval. Knots in quarter-sawed lumber frequently appear as long dagger-shaped defects that run across the grain, called spikes.

Wood is classified as either hardwood or softwood depending on the type of tree it came from. This classification has nothing to do with the actual hardness of the wood; softwoods are those from needle-bearing trees while hardwoods are from leaf-bearing trees. The actual hardness of the wood varies according to the species and the rate of growth. Generally, slow-growing trees produce harder wood than trees that grow rapidly. Hardness is of importance to the wood finisher because it plays a role in how stains and other finishing materials are absorbed.

There are many chemicals and trace minerals incorporated in the structure of wood. These elements are what give each wood its characteristic color. Tannin is a chemical that is present to a varying degree in most wood; it can create a large number of different color effects in combination with other chemicals. The finisher can take advantage of the natural chemical composition of wood to produce colors that are not natural for that species. By applying a chemical that will react with chemicals present in the wood, a variety of color effects can be produced.

As you work with woods you will begin to recognize the different characteristics described here and you will soon realize that each piece of wood has its own character that will affect the final appearance of any finish applied to it. It is this variability that gives wood its charm, but it also presents a challenge to the wood finisher. You can decide whether to accentuate the character of the wood or de-emphasize some feature. The creative finisher can use the individual characteristics of a piece of lumber to create an unusual effect or mask the character of one board so that the entire project will harmoniously blend together.

SAFETY FIRST

The process of finishing wood is inherently somewhat hazardous; but if you follow some common sense safety precautions, working with finishing materials can be safe and enjoyable. Many liquids used in finishing are flammable; don't smoke while using them. Use flammable liquids in a well-ventilated area away from pilot lights, arcing motors and switches or any other source of ignition. Always store flammable liquids in sealed containers, preferably the one originally supplied with the liquid or one approved for the storage of flammable liquids. Dispose of rags that have flammables on them in a tightly covered metal container to avoid spontaneous combustion.

Airborne dust from sanding or the overspray of spray equipment can pose a health hazard. To avoid inhaling harmful fumes open all windows and doors to ensure adequate ventilation. Turn on a fan and wear a dust mask or respirator when performing operations that produce dust or fumes. There are three main types of masks available; each has a specific use, and if the correct one is not used you will not be protected. The first type is the dust mask. This is simply a filter that fits over your nose and mouth; it will filter solid particles out of the air you breathe. It will not remove harmful vapors. The dust mask is sufficient protection from the dust produced by sanding. The next type is the organic vapor filter. This type uses a chemical cartridge to remove the vapors released by common finishing materials; many also incorporate a dust filter. This is the type most often used when spraying common finishing materials in a well-ventilated area. The third type is the air supplied respirator. This can be either a mask or a hood that covers your entire head. Fresh air is supplied by a hose to the respirator. This type is recommended when extremely toxic fumes are present or where adequate ventilation cannot be provided. The hood type has the advantage of protecting your eyes as well.

Eye protection is another important safety consideration. Goggles or a full face shield should be worn whenever caustic or irritating materials are being used. Eye protection is also necessary whenever there is a chance that a particle of wood or metal could be thrown into your eye; power sanding and tool sharpening are examples of this.

Neoprene gloves should be worn whenever your hands will come in direct contact with a finishing liquid or chemical stripper. Some of the solvents used can be very irritating to the skin. The more volatile solvents such as lacquer thinner are prone to remove the natural oil from your skin causing painful cracks to develop.

Chemicals, especially acids, have special precautions that should be followed. *Safety procedures for chemicals are fully discussed in the chapter on chemical stains.*

Because of the increased awareness of health problems posed by strong solvents, many new finishing products are being developed with a water base. These products are easy to use and provide good results.

Keep safety on your mind as you work and your enjoyment of wood finishing won't be marred by an accident.

1 · Wood Preparation

NEW WOOD

The first and one of the most vital steps in producing a fine finish on wood is wood preparation. If the wood is not smooth and free from blemishes, it will not finish well. Preparing wood to accept a finish begins as soon as the project is started.

One of the first steps in building any project from new wood project is squaring and surfacing the stock. If this procedure is not correctly done, the project is already doomed to have a second rate finish. As work on the project proceeds, other operations are performed that will have an effect on the final appearance of the finish. Assembling the pieces with glue is one operation that has a very derogatory affect on the final finish if it is not done carefully. Glue spots on the wood are difficult to remove and cause light areas in the finish that don't accept stain evenly. Sanding is another procedure that can make or break a fine finish.

Planing

Wood comes in several categories based on the degree of surfacing and jointing (preparation of the edge) that has been done at the mill. Rough wood hasn't been planed at all; it is just the way it left the saw. It may vary in thickness and the edges are neither square

with the face nor parallel with each other. Wood that has been planed on the faces is called S2S (surfaced two sides). It is uniform in thickness and both faces are parallel. The faces are smooth; all of the rough texture left by the saw has been removed. A board that has been jointed on both edges as well as having the faces surfaced is referred to as S4S (surfaced four sides). The edges are square with the face and parallel to each other.

In addition to the above types there are the following less commonly used varieties: S1S (surfaced one side), S1S1E (surfaced one side one edge), and S1S2E (surfaced one side two edges).

All of the above terms apply to solid lumber only. Plywood is available with the faces sanded or unsanded. Cabinet grades of plywood always come sanded and no further surfacing is required. Sanded plywood is ready for finish sanding as it comes from the mill.

The type of lumber you choose to use depends largely on what tools you have available. The more surfacing that is done by the mill the more you will have to pay for the lumber, but to use rough lumber you need a surface planer and a jointer.

A surface planer is one of the more expensive woodworking tools and will be found only in shops that do a large volume of work.

On the other hand, a jointer is almost a necessity in a serious woodworking shop. A jointer is all that is required to work with S2S lumber so you may find that using S2S is a practical way to save on lumber costs.

The Surface Planer. In addition to saving on the cost of lumber, surfacing your own lumber has several other advantages. First, you can vary the thickness of the lumber to suit the application. Second, if you keep your machine in good adjustment and use it carefully you can achieve a smoother surface than is common on most mill-surfaced lumber. At a mill, operations must be performed at the fastest speed that will produce satisfactory results. With both surfacing and jointing a slower feed speed will produce a smoother surface so the mill must compromise, but you don't have to.

As a wood finisher your objective, when using the planer, is to achieve the smoothest possible surface on the lumber being planed. A planer that is sharp and in good adjustment will produce good results if you feed at the proper speed and take grain direction into account. The cutting knives of a planer are set into a cylindrical head that rotates against the direction of feed. The cut made by the knives will be trough shaped because of the circular cutting motion. If the feed is slow enough, the troughs will be small and close together making them practically invisible and easy to remove. When the feed is too fast, the troughs will be large and easily discernible, creating a washboard effect. These marks are called mill marks. When this occurs it is much harder to achieve a smooth surface in later finishing steps. Roughing cuts to bring the stock close to the desired thickness can be made at a faster speed and cutting about ⅛ in. at a time. For the final finishing cut, slow the feed down and only take a ¹⁄₁₆ in. cut.

If the grain in the board you are planing angles up into the direction of the cutter rota-

tion, small chips or tears may appear in the surface of the stock. If you notice this occurring on the first rough cut, turn the board end for end, so it is feeding in the opposite direction for all of the subsequent cuts. Sometimes the grain direction will change part way through a board; this is especially true around knots. If the full length of the board isn't needed, cut it at the point the grain changes so that each piece can be fed in the proper direction. If this is not practical, take very shallow cuts at a slow feed to reduce the chipping.

You should achieve good results by following these directions if the planer is operating correctly. If you don't get a smooth surface then the fault is probably in the adjustment or maintenance of the machine. There are five parts of the planer that commonly produce an unacceptable surface when they are not maintained or adjusted properly. They are the in-feed rollers, the chip breaker, pressure bar, out-feed rollers, and the cutter head. (Illus. 4, 5)

The in-feed rollers feed the stock into the machine; the upper in-feed roller is serrated

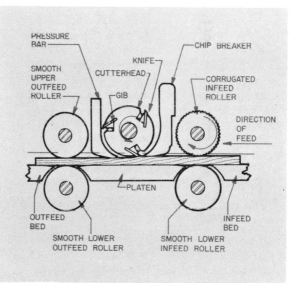

Illus. 4. **The major internal parts of the surface planer.**

17

Illus. 5. This planer is designed to eliminate many of the adjustments necessary on most machines. It uses rubber feed rollers that don't require any adjustment and there are no lower feed rollers; instead, the table is made of polished stainless steel.

to grip the stock. These serrations scar the wood, but since the planer removes the top surface of the board as it travels through the machine, it doesn't matter. Some machines use a rubber roller instead of a serrated metal one.

The chip breaker presses against the surface of the board directly in front of the cutter head. If the chip breaker were absent, the cutting knives would tear long chips out of the surface of the board. The chip breaker breaks the chips before they have a chance to tear.

The pressure bar is positioned directly behind the cutter head and holds the stock firmly against the bed.

The out-feed rollers help to pull the board through the machine. They are most necessary when the end of the board has passed the in-feed rollers. Both out-feed rollers are smooth because they press directly on the planed surface. If a recurring defect appears in the same general location evenly spaced along the surface of the board, look for a nick or accumulation of pitch on the out-feed rollers.

The cutter head houses the cutting knives. They must be kept properly sharpened and jointed or poor results will occur.

One of the most common problems that improper adjustment may cause is a snipe at one end of the board. A snipe is an area of the board that has been cut deeper than the rest of the surface. If the snipe occurs at the end that was fed into the planer, the most likely cause is a chip breaker that is set too high. Other likely causes are a lower in-feed roller that is too high, a pressure bar that is set too low or with not enough spring tension, or an upper in-feed roll that is set too high. A snipe at the end that fed through the planer last is usually caused by a pressure bar that is set too high. When the lower out-feed roller is set too high or the upper out-feed roller set too low, a snipe will also result.

Chips, scars, and marks left by the planer are a more serious problem to the wood finisher. At least snipes can be cut off and discarded before the board is put to use, but some scars left by an improperly sharpened or damaged blade run the entire length of the board.

A raised line running with the length of the board indicates a chip or nick in the blades. It may also indicate that the blades have been improperly sharpened in the past. If the blades were allowed to burn during the grinding process they will lose their temper and nicks will form easily. This type of blemish is fairly easy to correct in later finishing operations since it is raised above the rest of the surface.

A nick that is gouged below the surface is much harder to remove later so it should be corrected immediately at the source. A gouge running parallel to the length of the board may be caused by a dragging pressure bar or by an accumulation of wood chips stuck between the out-feed roller and the bed.

Irregularly shaped dents that occur at random spots on the board are caused by wood chips that are pressed into the surface by the out-feed rollers. To correct this problem check the exhaust system. If it is clogged it won't remove all of the chips and some will fall back to the surface of the board.

Regularly spaced dents that seem to be in a line along most of the length of the board are caused by accumulations of pitch or wood chips mixed with pitch that are stuck to one of the out-feed rollers or the lower in-feed roller, or by a defect in the surface of one of these rollers.

A burn mark across the width of the board indicates that the board stuck at that point momentarily. This may have been caused by taking too heavy a cut or it may mean that the in-feed or out-feed rollers don't have enough tension.

Chips or areas of raised grain may indicate that the blades need to be sharpened and jointed. Also if a washboard effect occurs even when the feed speed is set correctly, dull blades may be the cause.

The Abrasive Planer.   Most of the problems associated with machine planing can be eliminated by using an abrasive planer. An abrasive planer is basically a wide belt sander with a feed mechanism similar to a planer. Industrial models have opposing heads that smooth both sides of the lumber at once. (Illus. 6) Smaller models are available that surface one side at a time.

Since the wood is sanded away rather than cut, grain direction and knots don't create the problems that they do with a conventional planer. This fact has made abrasive

Illus. 6. An abrasive planer uses wide sanding belts instead of knives to smooth the lumber's surface. The opposing heads on this machine surface both sides of the board at once.

planing popular in industry because it cuts down on waste. Another factor that makes abrasive planing attractive in an industrial setting is that maintenance is much simpler, decreasing downtime. The fact that more mills are switching to abrasive planing is a boon to wood finishers because the lumber produced requires much less preparation. Mill marks, raised grain, tear outs, snipes, and gouges are practically absent from lumber surfaced with an abrasive planer. (Illus. 7) If you use abrasive planed lumber you can usually go directly to the finish sanding operation.

The Jointer.   The jointer's main function is to produce a smooth square edge on a piece of lumber. It can also be used to surface

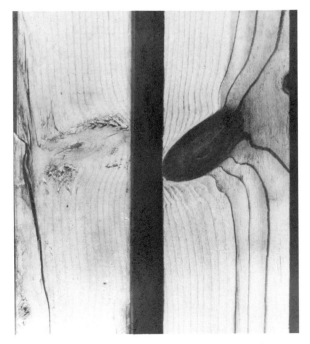

Illus. 7. The board on the left was planed with a conventional planer. Notice the mill marks, raised grain and chips around the knot. The board on the right, surfaced with an abrasive planer, is free of them.

Hand Planes. Any board that has been surfaced with a conventional power planer or jointer, no matter how well adjusted the tool was, will have a slight washboard surface. This is unavoidable with a rotating cutter head. So whether you buy lumber that was surfaced at the mill or surface it yourself, you will have to remove these mill marks.

A hand plane is the best way to remove mill marks; however, a belt sander can also be used on boards with only slightly apparent marks. A plane shaves a thin slice of wood off the face of the board. Since the bottom of the plane is very long in relation to the width of one of the troughs left by the planer cutter head, it spans many of the marks, riding only on the peaks. This means that the blade is kept at a uniform depth, creating a smooth surface free of the washboard ridges caused by the rotating cutter. Hand planes come in many sizes ranging from the short block plane to the very long jointer plane. All of the sizes serve useful purposes in woodwork, but for the purposes described here, a jack plane which is from 11½ in. to 15 in. long or a smooth plane which is 7 in. to 9 in. long will work best. (Illus. 8, 9)

Illus. 8. A jack plane.

one face of a board as long as the cutter head of the jointer is wider than the board. A jointer is useful for surfacing a face because it will remove slight twisting and warping while a planer won't.

Surface defects caused by an improperly adjusted or maintained jointer are similar to those found with the planer. A washboard effect is caused by too fast a feed. Since there is no feed mechanism on a jointer, the feed is controlled solely by how fast you push the board across the cutter. If the edge is not smooth enough, simply push slower. You can even vary the speed that you push the board to accommodate defects and changes in grain direction.

A nick in the blade creates the same characteristic raised line that was described for the planer. Dull blades will cause chipping and raised grain.

A snipe at the end of the board is caused by the out-feed table being adjusted too low.

The blade should be sharp and slightly rounded at the corners. The corners are rounded to prevent them from digging into the wood. Don't go overboard when round-

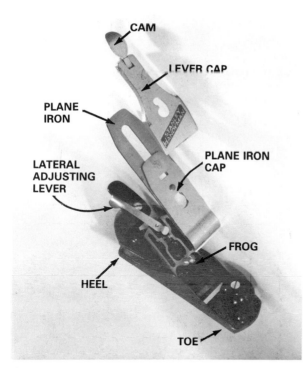

Illus. 9. Plane, exploded view.

Labels on diagram:
CAM
LEVER CAP
PLANE IRON
PLANE IRON CAP
LATERAL ADJUSTING LEVER
FROG
HEEL
TOE

motion for another inch or two before lifting the plane. Go back to the other end of the board and begin another pass slightly overlapping the first. Continue in this manner until the entire face has been planed. (Illus. 10)

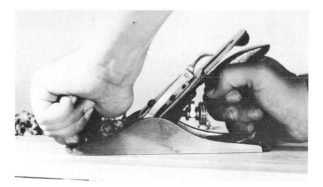

Illus. 10. Using a plane to remove mill marks.

ing the corners or a noticeable dip in the board will be produced; slightly rounded means that the rounding is difficult even to see. Set the plane iron cap to 1/32 in. from the tip of the blade and adjust the plane for a very shallow cut; use the lateral adjusting lever to set the blade square in the slot.

Place the board on a bench with its end against a bench stop or a bench hook with the grain facing away from you. You will be planing "with the grain" to avoid chips and roughening. Place the toe of the plane on the end of the board opposite the bench stop and turn the plane about 10 degrees in relation to the length of the board. Now apply gentle pressure to the toe and advance the plane into the work. When the blade has cleared the end of the board by about an inch, slightly increase the downward pressure on the plane. Continue along the entire length of the face in a smooth even stroke. When the blade clears the end of the board, release downward pressure but continue forward

A hand plane works best on even grained wood without many knots. Knots or a wild grain will cause the plane to dig in and chip the wood. In that case the planing is causing more harm than good. Problem boards are best handled with a belt sander.

Scrapers. It's a sad fact that scrapers have fallen into general disuse lately. Many new woodworkers have never seen or used one. Even though they may be hard to find, a good cabinet scraper and a hand scraper will be a wise investment for anyone serious about producing a topnotch finish. (Illus. 11)

Illus. 11. Left, cabinet scraper. Right, hand scraper.

A sharp scraper in the hands of an experienced worker can produce a surface so smooth that it's hard to duplicate even with very fine sandpaper. (Illus. 12)

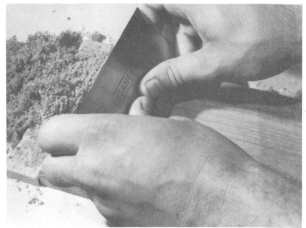

Illus. 13. Apply thumb pressure to the center of the hand scraper to give the blade a slight bow.

Illus. 12. Using a cabinet scraper.

It's important to keep a scraper sharp; a dull scraper doesn't work at all. The procedure for sharpening a scraper seems a bit strange to someone who has never seen it done before; but once you've learned how, it's not hard.

In use, a scraper blade should have a slight bow sprung into it. With the cabinet scraper this is accomplished by turning an adjustment screw that presses against the center of the blade while the edges of the blade are held secure by the frame. With a hand scraper you must bow the blade with your hands. Grasp the blade with both hands. Position your fingers around the edges and thumbs pressing against the middle of the blade. Press in with your thumbs to give the blade a slight bow. (Illus. 13)

The bowed-out center of the blade should cut first; this means that you must push a hand scraper away from you, pushing mostly with your thumbs. The cabinet scraper can be either pushed or pulled, but always keep the blade facing so that the bowed out center cuts first.

The scraper will produce a very thin shaving, not dust as sandpaper will. Always work the scraper with the grain. Overlap strokes

as you proceed across the face of the board. As soon as the scraper shows signs of becoming dull, resharpen it.

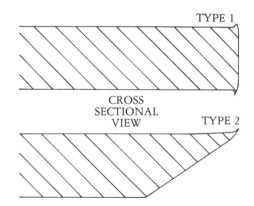

Illus. 14. The cross-sectional views at the top show the difference between a hand scraper blade (Type 1) and a cabinet scraper blade (Type 2).

The actual cutting edge of a scraper is a small burr that is formed on the edge of the blade. (Illus. 14) To prepare the blade to accept a new burr, place the blade in a vise whose jaws have been padded with wood blocks. Remove the old burr by filing across the face edge. Next, draw a smooth millfile across the edge, holding it perfectly flat and square on a hand scraper and holding it at

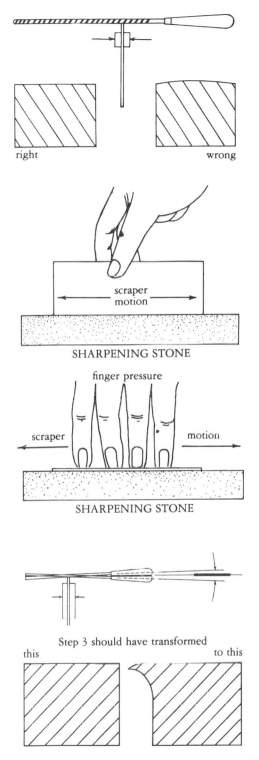

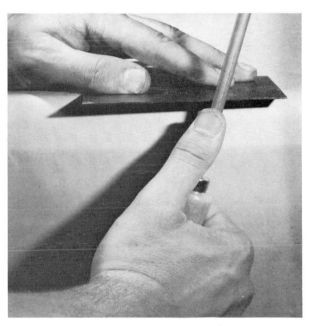

Illus. 15. Step 1 in sharpening a scraper is to file the edge square. Whetting the edge on a sharpening stone is step 2. Forming the burr with a burnisher is step 3.

the same angle as presently exists on a cabinet scraper blade (approximately 45 degrees). Slightly round the corners. Next, use a whetstone to whet the edge. Hold the blade of a hand scraper square with the stone; hold the bevelled side of a cabinet scraper blade against the stone as you would to sharpen a plane iron. Turn the blade on its side holding it flat against the surface of the stone and rub it back and forth several times to remove the burr left from whetting the edge. (Illus. 15)

To form the cutting burr you will need a burnisher. There are tools made specifically for the purpose but any hardened tool steel object can be used. A lathe gouge or an awl will work well. Place the blade on a table with the cutting edge protruding about ½ in. past the table edge. (Illus. 16) Put a drop of

Illus. 16. Using a burnisher to form a burr.

oil on the burnisher and rub it over the entire surface. Holding the burnisher flat against the surface of the blade, draw it along the edge about four times. For the hand scraper the next step is to position the burnisher so it is square with the face of the blade riding along the edge. Draw the burnisher towards you once and then tilt the burnisher slightly and draw it across the edge again. Take about three or four more strokes across the edge, tilting it a little more each time until the final stroke is made with the burnisher held at about 85 degrees to the face of the blade. To burnish a cabinet scraper blade, start by holding the burnisher at about 45 degrees and increase the angle on each subsequent stroke until an angle of about 75 degrees is reached.

When the blade becomes dull it is not necessary to file and whet the edge every time; simply repeat the burnishing process. When you can't get a good burr by burnishing alone, then file and whet the edge.

Scrapers also are useful for smoothing a shaped edge. You can purchase a ready-made scraper that is shaped so that different areas of the edge will fit the contours of various size coves. If there is a particular shaped edge (a roman ogee for example) that you encounter frequently, you can grind one corner of a hand scraper to fit that shape. As you grind, take small cuts and keep the blade cool by frequently dipping it in water, otherwise the blade will burn and lose its temper.

Gluing

Assembling the parts of a project with glue can affect the finish because glue acts as a sealer that will prevent subsequent finishing materials from penetrating into the wood. If glue is smeared on the face of a board and not completely removed, a lighter-colored blemish will appear in the finish.

The best way to avoid glue spots in the finish is to prevent glue from ever coming in contact with the surface of the work. Careful assembly can eliminate most problems. Practice gluing scraps until you are able to gauge how much glue to spread on a joint. For a strong joint there should be just enough glue

so that a tiny bead of glue is formed all along the joint when it is clamped tight. If you use too much glue it will drip and ooze over the face. If too little glue is used the joint will be weak, so it is important to use just the right amount of glue.

Many people make the mistake of trying to wipe off wet glue. This only creates further problems because it spreads the glue around and forces it into the pores of the wood. It's even a bigger mistake to use a damp rag to wipe off glue because the water in the rag will thin the glue and allow it to penetrate even further into the wood. The best way to remove glue is to let it dry and then shave it from the surface using a sharp chisel or scraper. If you have used the right amount of glue so that a very small bead squeezes from the joint, it can be easily and completely removed by letting it dry and shaving it off with a chisel. Always remove glue with a chisel or scraper before sanding; the heat generated by sanding tends to soften glue marks and spread them around. What started as a small glue mark can turn into a large dirty looking smudge if it is sanded before the glue is removed. White glue (Polyvinyl acetate) is especially apt to smear when sanded.

Care must also be taken in the way you clamp a joint. Always use a pad of wood or cork between the clamp and any wood surfaces that will receive a finish. The bare clamp can dent the wood and leave stains. When wet glue comes in contact with an iron clamp a black stain appears on the wood. This type of stain is very hard to remove because it is actually a chemical change in the wood itself; the only effective way to remove it is to scrape, plane or sand the wood away until the stain is gone. Wood hand screws, especially new ones, will leave an oil spot where they come in contact with the wood. You can sometimes remove an oil stain like this by mixing blackboard chalk dust with water and applying the paste to the stain. Let the paste dry and scrape it off. If may be necessary to repeat the process several times.

Dents caused by clamping without pads can sometimes be removed by applying a little water to the dent. If that doesn't work, wet the area again and apply a hot iron to the area. Don't keep the iron in one spot too long or it will burn the wood. Dents must be removed in this manner or they will cause trouble later. If, for example, you choose to plane the edge to remove the dent, the area that is dented will expand later when a finish is applied and cause a raised area. This is because the wood fibers in the dented area are compressed while the surrounding fibers are not. If you plane off the surrounding wood to the same level as the dent, the dented area actually contains more wood fibers than the surrounding wood. Of course, if you can take off a lot of wood without affecting the project, you can plane out a dent; just make sure that you plane deep enough to remove all of the compressed fibers.

Filling Nail Holes and Defects

Whenever possible, it's best to avoid having any nail holes in a visible surface, but when it's unavoidable the nails should be set about ⅛ in. below the surface and the hole filled. Small cracks and knotholes should also be filled.

Fillers for this use come in two basic types: solvent-based and water-based. The solvent-based fillers are commonly called plastic putty or wood dough. This type shrinks slightly as it dries so you should leave it slightly bumped up when you apply it. Solvent-based putty will seal any wood that it touches so it will leave a mark similar to a glue mark. For this reason you should be very careful how you apply the putty or there will be unsightly marks around the nail holes. Use a small straight-blade screwdriver or the point of a pocketknife to push a small

amount of putty into the hole. Try not to smear any of the putty on the surrounding wood. When the putty has dried, sand it flush with the surrounding surface. Plastic putty is available in several colors that match different varieties of wood. It is important to use a color that will match the intended finish, because this type of putty won't accept stain very well; so even if the bare wood is light colored, use a dark colored putty if the final finish will be dark.

The other type of putty is water based. You mix just the amount of dry powder with water that will do the job at hand because the putty will harden in less than one hour. In its natural state this type of putty is light tan to white. You can color the putty to any shade you wish by mixing it with dry water stain. This type of putty won't shrink as it dries. It will also accept a stain better than plastic putty. Sometimes it will absorb the stain so well that it will be considerably darker than the wood around it. In that case you may have to use a small artist's brush to apply a small drop of shellac to the putty before applying the stain. Apply it in the same manner described for plastic putty. It won't cause as noticeable a mark if it gets on the wood surface but you should still try to avoid smearing it around.

Nail holes can also be filled after the finish has been applied. To do this you use a product called a filler stick. Filler sticks are similar to a fat crayon in appearance and are made of a colored waxy substance. Choose a stick that closely matches the color of the finish; if you can't get an exact match, a filler that is slightly darker will be less noticeable than one that is lighter. Rub the point of the filler stick over the nail hole until the hole is filled; then polish the surrounding surface with a clean rag to remove the putty that was deposited on the surface. This method is easy and fast but the putty will always remain soft, so it should only be used in small holes that are located inconspicuously.

Sanding

Sanding is probably the most familiar form of smoothing a wood surface. Sanding smooths the wood by using sharp pieces of grit to cut the wood fibers. Just as a broken piece of glass has a sharp edge that can be used as a wood scraper so do the abrasive particles. They are made of substances that fracture like glass. When they are crushed to the proper size they fracture, producing the sharp edges that cut the wood. When you use sandpaper you are in effect using thousands of tiny scrapers at one time. (Illus. 17) Many times the sanding operation is overused because the preceding steps were overlooked or done poorly. When the wood has been properly planed and scraped, sanding will be neither laborious nor time consuming.

Coated abrasive is the proper name for all products that consist of an abrasive material bonded to a backing. Technically speaking, the term sandpaper only applies to flint paper; however, it has commonly come to mean any coated abrasive with a paper backing. In this book the term sandpaper will be used to describe all coated abrasives with paper backing regardless of the abrasive used. Coated abrasives with a cloth backing are referred to as "abrasive cloth."

Types of Abrasives. There are two major classifications of abrasives used in sandpaper: natural and man-made. The natural abrasives are flint, garnet, and emery. The man-made abrasives are aluminum oxide and silicon carbide.

Flint has been used for sandpaper longer than any of the other abrasives. It is a naturally occurring mineral that has the appearance of yellowish-white sand. Flintpaper is usually less expensive than any other type of sandpaper, but it also wears out faster than any other type so it may turn out to be more expensive in the long run.

Garnet is another natural abrasive. It is much harder than flint, so it can keep cutting much longer. Garnet has a tendency to fracture during use so it keeps producing new cutting points. You can recognize garnet by its reddish yellow color.

Emery usually comes on a cloth backing and is generally used for cleaning metal. It can be used on wood; the flexible cloth backing makes it useful for smoothing contoured surfaces. It is harder than garnet; but because it doesn't fracture as easily, it won't renew its cutting surface like some of the other abrasives. You can recognize emery by its black color.

Aluminum oxide is a man-made material made in an electric furnace. Sandpaper coated with aluminum oxide lasts longer than garnet. Because of its long life and good cutting properties, aluminum oxide is probably the best abrasive for woodwork. Even though it is more expensive than flint or garnet, it is well worth the cost. Whenever

Illus. 17. **These microscopic photos of abrasive particles show how the fractures form sharp cutting edges.**

26

sandpaper is specified in this book, aluminum oxide is the abrasive recommended unless otherwise noted.

Most companies use a trade name for the man-made abrasives rather than the generic name. This can make it a little confusing when you are looking for aluminum oxide paper. You can usually recognize aluminum oxide by its reddish-brown color. Sometimes aluminum oxide paper will be variegated grey or white; this is caused by a special coating applied to prevent the paper from clogging. If you are in doubt as to the abrasive used in a particular paper, ask the salesperson.

Silicon carbide is harder than even aluminum oxide. For wood finishing, it is primarily used in only the finest grades to sand between coats of a finish. Silicon carbide paper is a very uniform blue-black color.

Grit Sizes. There are three systems of designating grit size. The first system gives a name to the different degrees of fineness, starting with coarse and proceding through medium, fine, very fine, and extra fine. This system is not very precise because one term, such as medium, may actually refer to several grit sizes within the medium range. Normally this system is used in conjunction with one of the other systems to give someone unfamiliar with the more precise systems a general idea of the grit size; however, in the case of flint paper, many times the fineness name will be the only designation given.

The second system is the aught system. It is so called because most of the grades are designated by a number of zeros or aughts. In this system the coarsest grit is a 4; the smaller the number is, the finer the grit. Sizes smaller than zero are designated by additional zeros. Most of the grades useful in wood finishing fall in this category. For example, a fine grit sandpaper might be designated 4/0 (read four aught). You may also see 4/0 written as 0000.

The third system is the most versatile because it allows for more grades than the other two. It is called the mesh system. In this system the number designates the number of holes per square inch in a mesh screen used to sort the abrasive granules. The higher the number, the finer the grit. Grit sizes usually used in woodwork range from 50 as the coarsest to 600 as the finest. Throughout this book sandpaper grades will be given in the mesh system because this is the one in widest use.

Coating. Sandpaper can clog with gummy varnish, glue, or resins from the wood. Clogging decreases the useful life of the sandpaper considerably. For this reason, sandpaper is available in closed- and open-coat as well as with a special non-clog coating.

Closed-coat means that the entire surface of the paper is covered with grit. This is the fastest cutting type of paper if you are using it on bare hardwood.

Open-coat sandpaper has spaces of bare paper around each grit. This type is much slower to clog than closed-coat paper, so even though there are fewer granules of grit it will cut faster and last longer when you are sanding finished surfaces or softwoods.

Some companies offer a special coating that reduces clogging. This coating is what gives some paper a white or grey color.

While sanding, occasionally slap the sandpaper against a hard surface to remove the accumulated dust from between the grit. When sanding a finished surface, small circular accumulations of the finish will stick to the paper; remove them with your fingernail or a knife blade as soon as they form. If they are not removed, they can scar the surface. They also reduce the cutting efficiency of the paper.

Backing. Coated abrasives are applied to several types of backings. Paper comes in several weights. The weight of the paper is designated by a letter of the alphabet with A being the lightest weight paper. The weights usually used in wood finishing are A, C, and D. Sometimes paper with an A weight backing is referred to as finishing paper, while C and D weight papers are called cabinet paper. The heavier stock is not very flexible, but it will withstand heavy use. Unless you special-order your sandpaper in large quantities, you will have to settle for the weight of paper that the manufacturer has decided is best for most jobs in each particular grit size. Generally coarse grits come on heavier paper.

Cloth is another popular backing. It comes in several weights. Jeans (J) and Drills (X) are the most commonly used for general woodwork. Most sheets come with a Jeans backing; it is strong and flexible. Sanding belts usually are made of Drills. Heavier weights like Y and M are used for abrasive planer belts.

Cloth-backed abrasives are useful for sanding irregular surfaces and getting into small crevices. Cloth backing is very useful in power sanding because it resists tearing.

Screen-backed abrasives offer the ultimate in non-clogging. The abrasive is applied to fiberglass screen. Both sides of the screen are coated so you can turn it over for a fresh surface.

Discs and drums are made of a fibre backing that is similar to very strong cardboard.

Wet-or-dry Paper. The adhesive used to attach the grit to the paper is usually not waterproof in standard types of sandpaper. Wet-or-dry paper uses a special waterproof adhesive as well as a waterproof backing paper. This allows you to sand a surface that is wet. This feature is very useful in wood finishing when sanding finish coats. For example, when sanding the final coat of a lacquer finish in preparation for rubbing, a little water will lubricate the surface and also prevent the sandpaper from clogging.

Flex. The glue used to attach the abrasive to the backing cures hard and inflexible. When the backing is bent, the glue will crack. It is desirable for these cracks in the glue to be uniformly spaced and formed in the proper direction if the material is to have the desired flexibility and life. For this reason, a coated abrasive should be preflexed. For sheets, this operation is performed by the user. Abrasive belts are mechanically flexed at the factory in a variety of patterns to fit the intended use. (Illus. 18)

Arrow indicates the lengthwise direction of the belt, roll or sheet.

Noflex:
No mechanical flex. This unflexed or stiff construction is furnished as standard in items such as sheets, in fine grade paper products for hand or machine sanding where added flexibility is not desirable or necessary.

Singlflex:
A single mechanical flex which creates flex lines at 90° to the edge or running direction of the material. This flexing provides a minimum handling flex and the necessary conformability to run over even small diameter pulleys and contact wheels.

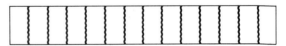

Doublflex:
(2-45° angle flexes). Two mechanical flexing operations which make the material moderately flexible in all directions.

Fulflex:
(2.45° angles and a 90° angle flex). Three mechanical flexes resulting in a product that is soft and flexible, regardless of the direction in which it must bend or conform.

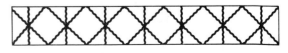

Illus. 18. Types of flexes.

Sanding Technique. Scraping and planing will usually leave small ridges that must be removed before a finish can be applied. These ridges are removed by sanding. If you have properly planed and scraped the lumber, the sanding operation won't be too difficult.

In the first phase of sanding your goal is to flatten out any irregularities left on the surface of the board. To do this you need to use a nonflexible sanding block. A piece of hardwood works well. If you tear a sheet of sandpaper into quarters you can use a sanding block that is 3 in. × 5 in. × ¾ in. This size allows the paper to slightly overhang lengthwise and fold over enough so you can get a good grip on the paper. The face of the block should be flat and free of any irregularities. To achieve this, lay a piece of 100 grit sandpaper, grit up, on a surface that is machined flat such as a saw table. If you don't have a machined surface, the best substitute is a plastic laminate table top. Hold the sandpaper stationary with one hand and rub the sanding block across the paper until all surface irregularities have been removed.

The first grade of sandpaper to use depends on the condition of the surface to be sanded. If you have planed and scraped the surface, don't use anything coarser than 100. If you've done a very good job of scraping you can start with 180. The main idea is to use the grade that will remove the remaining defects effectively without causing too much damage to the smooth parts of the surface already achieved through scraping.

When you have decided what grit size to use, fold the sheet into quarters then tear along the fold lines. Next, flex the paper, place it grit side up on the edge of a table and pull it down across the edge. Turn it one quarter turn and repeat. This process forms many small cracks in the glue that holds the grit on. This way you prevent large cracks from developing in the glue as you sand, thus increasing the life of the paper.

Illus. 19. A hardwood block used with the first grade of sandpaper will help to remove any remaining surface irregularities. Notice that the folded edge of the sandpaper faces the direction of travel. This helps to prevent the edge of the sandpaper from catching on the wood and tearing.

Fold the paper around the block and grip the edges with your thumb on one edge and your fingers on the other. Position the block on the board so that the folded edges are at a 90 degree angle to the direction of travel. This helps prevent tearing the paper. (Illus. 19) Apply moderate pressure to the paper and sand with the grain of the wood. Apply equal pressure on both the forward and back stroke. Some people tend to apply the most pressure on the forward stroke and release the pressure on the back stroke. This tends to comb down the wood fibres in one direction. Later as the finish is applied these combed down fibres can raise up and create a rough or fuzzy surface. By sanding in both directions the protruding fibres will be cut off flush with the surface, so there will be less fuzzing when the finish is applied. Be careful while you are sanding with the hardwood block; if any particles of wood or grit accumulate between the sandpaper and the block, they can cause that area to sand deeper than the rest. You should avoid sanding across the grain because this will cut the fibres of the wood. When stain is applied to the wood the cut ends of the fibres will ab-

Illus. 20. This type of sanding block is useful for sanding flat surfaces. It has a hard backing and only a slight amount of padding. This particular model uses a roll of self-adhesive sandpaper. When a section becomes dull, it is torn off and a new section pulled from the roll.

Illus. 21. A sanding block with a soft backing is used to follow any remaining surface variations.

sorb more than the surrounding wood and show up as dark scratches. Sometimes it is necessary to sand across the grain; this is especially true with turnings. In that case start with a finer grade sandpaper than you would normally use. The last grade you use should also be finer than normal. This will minimize the scratch marks, but they will still be visible upon close examination. Remove all defects in the board with the coarsest grit you are going to use; all of the subsequent sanding is to remove the scratches left by the preceding grit, not to remove defects.

When you are satisfied with the surface, you can switch to the next finer grit. Taking small jumps in grit size is actually faster than trying to go from a coarse grit to a much finer one in one step, because a grit that is only slightly smaller than the preceding one will cut much faster than one that is a lot smaller. For example, if you start with 100 you will have better results if you go to 150 before you use 180.

After you have removed all defects with the first grade of paper, you should use a flexible sanding block for the subsequent grades. You can use a commercially available block or make your own by padding a wood block with cork or felt. There are several reasons for using a padded block. First, the padding protects the surface you have already achieved from being damaged by any particles that get wedged between the paper and the block. Second, the flexible backing allows even pressure to be applied to the surface even if there are some irregularities left. A padded block also protects the sandpaper, making it last longer. There are many types of commercial blocks; some are designed for specific purposes. A block with a solid backing and only a moderate amount of padding is best for sanding flat surfaces. (Illus. 20) A soft block with a semi-flexible backing is useful when using the finest grades of sandpaper. The flexible block allows the paper to contact the entire surface even if there are slight dips or bumps. (Illus. 21) For touch-up sanding and sanding irregularly shaped objects, a pad with a soft flexible backing is best. (Illus. 22).

As you sand with the finer grades your only objective is to replace the larger

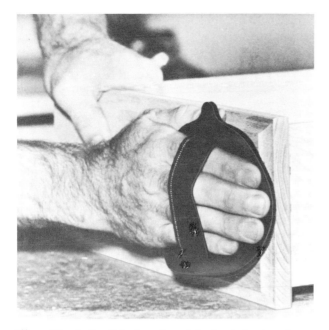

Illus. 22. A flexible hand pad is best for touch-up sanding and for sanding odd-shaped objects.

scratches left by the preceding grade with smaller ones made by the grade you are using. Once you have achieved this, switch to the next finer grade.

When to stop sanding depends on what type of final finish you are after. If the surface will be painted, you can stop with 150. Most surfaces to be varnished or lacquered should be sanded with 220. If you are after the ultimate finish, you may want to go to 320 or 400; but keep in mind that grits finer than 220 tend to give the wood a burnished effect that is desirable in some cases but not in others. You should take the type of finish to be applied into account when you sand the wood. The burnished surface produces a beautifully polished look when a penetrating oil finish is used. But in some cases the burnishing will make the wood take stain unevenly, so be sure to try a sample if you want to use the finer grades of sandpaper. The burnished surface is more apparent when using a power sander, so you can usually use a finer grit when hand sanding than you could use with a power sander.

If you will be using a water-based stain, you need to perform one additional sanding step. Wipe a wet sponge over the wood surface; then using wet-or-dry paper one grade finer than the paper you used last, sand the surface smooth. Instead of sanding directly with the grain, sand at about a five degree angle to the grain direction. This slight deviation from the grain direction won't create cross grain scratches and it will cut off the fibres better. Wet the surface again and sand it. This process will smooth off the fibres that rise up when they get wet, so when you apply the stain the surface will dry smooth.

Finally, after all other sanding is complete, use fine sandpaper to remove the sharp edge from the corners. Don't round the corners unless the design calls for it; just pass the sanding block along the edge once or twice to get rid of the sharp corner. Removing the sharp edge will make the finish last longer on the edges. If it is not removed the finish will quickly wear off at the corners leaving a visibly lighter line.

Power Sanders. Although power sanders are one of the safer power tools, you still need to exercise the same caution you would with any other power tool. Don't wear loose clothing or dangling sleeves, and if you have long hair, tie it back. If your clothing or hair gets caught in a rotating pulley, it will draw you into the machine. For the same reason you should avoid wearing loose gloves around power equipment. Power sanders kick up more dust than hand sanding does, so whenever possible connect the sander to an exhaust system or shop vacuum. Wear a dust mask to avoid inhaling the dust, and protect your eyes with goggles. Whenever you change the abrasive, disconnect the sander from the power source.

There are several types of power sanders available to make the job of sanding easier. Each has advantages and disadvantages.

The *belt sander* has the advantage of removing a lot of wood quickly and producing sanding marks that are parallel to the grain. Its major drawback is that it may remove the wood too quickly and cause irregularities in the surface if it is not used carefully. Also, belt sanders are more expensive than other types.

Belt sanders use an abrasive belt that varies in length and width according to the type of machine. (Illus. 23) Portable belt sanders are the most common but stationary models are available. The portable belt sander uses a belt between about 14 in. and 30 in. in length and three in. and five in. in width. The belt travels over two rollers, one at each end of the machine. One of the rollers is connected to the motor to move the belt; the other is spring loaded to tension the belt. (Illus. 24)

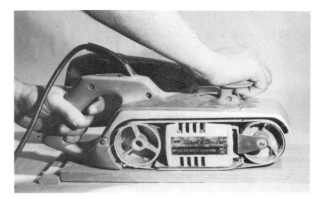

Illus. 24. A belt sander is a very efficient way to sand, but you must use it correctly to prevent it from damaging the surface. Hold the sander with two hands. Apply even pressure to the base and don't tilt it; keep the sander moving, don't let it remain in one place.

you are careful with it, a belt sander will produce very good results; however, it takes practice to get the feel of one, so start on scrap wood to learn how to handle one. The major problem novices have with a belt sander is they leave it in one spot too long, creating a dip; or they tilt it causing one side of the belt to cut deeper than the other, creating a gouge. For this reason even a seasoned pro should be careful when using a belt sander on an important surface. Because a

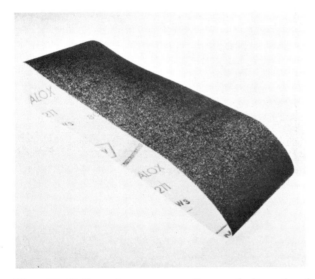

Illus. 23. Belt sanders use a continuous belt made of cloth-backed abrasive.

To use a portable belt sander correctly, you must always keep it flat against the work and apply even pressure to it without tilting the base. Always move the sander with the direction of the grain. If possible, sand the whole length of the board before moving side to side. Occasionally reverse the direction of sanding to cut off any combed down fibers. If

Illus. 25. A scroll sander is useful for sanding edges. Its design permits it to be used to sand the inside edges of cut-out areas.

32

Illus. 26. Shaped edges can be sanded using a special belt sander and a mould block that is made to fit the contour of the edge.

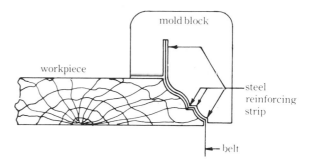

Illus. 27. This cross-section shows how the mould block shapes the belt to fit the contours of the edge. Steel reinforcing strips protect the block from wear.

belt sander cuts so fast, don't use it to sand plywood or veneers until you are thoroughly sure of how to operate the machine. It's very easy to sand right through the face veneer without even knowing it.

As was stated earlier, a belt sander can be used to remove the mill marks left by a planer. Use a coarse 50 or 60 grit belt. Be sure to remove all of the marks before changing to a finer belt.

One type of belt sander that is very useful for sanding intricate shapes is the *scroll sander.* (Illus. 25) The scroll sander uses a very narrow belt. The belt extends vertically from the table and passes over a small roller that is supported several inches above the table. This type has the capability of sanding inside of openings. Another type of sander that is used similarly is the *band saw sanding belt.* This is a belt that fits on a band saw the same as the band saw blade. It is useful for edge sanding intricately cut parts, but it cannot be used to sand inside of an opening as the scroll sander can.

A type of stationary belt sander that can rival hand sanding for ease of control and quality of work is the *hand block belt sander.* The hand block belt sander uses a very long belt (several feet long). The work is placed on a movable table and the belt is directly over the work. A block similar to a hand sanding block is pressed against the back of the belt to

bring the belt in contact with the work. The position of the block and the pressure applied can be varied as easily as with hand sanding. A variation on the hand block sander uses shaped blocks to contour the belt. This type is used to sand mouldings and shaped edges. (Illus. 26, 27)

The *backstand sander* has one roller exposed. All sanding takes place on this roller. This type is used for freehand sanding of curved parts like chair legs. (Illus. 28)

One very specialized form of belt sander is the *drawer sander.* (Illus. 29) This type will usually only be found in shops that produce a large number of drawers. The drawer sander is useful for fitting drawers that have

Illus. 28. Backstand sanders are used for freehand sanding of curved surfaces.

Illus. 29. A drawer sander is for sanding inside corners.

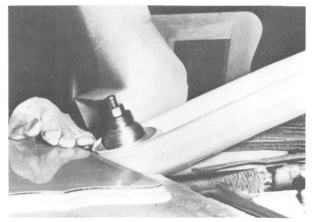

Illus. 30. Spool and belt sanders use a flexible belt and a shaped spool to sand complex edge shapes.

Illus. 31. A DeLappe sander can be made in a small shop to handle a limited production run that requires shaped edge sanding.

a face that extends past the side. The belt must make a sharp 90 degree turn to sand the square inside corner of the drawer. This sharp turn is very hard on the belt and the platen that supports it. The edge of the platen is made of a special ceramic material that can withstand the friction and wear generated when the belt rubs over it.

Another type of sander that will sand a shaped edge is the *spool and belt sander*. (Illus. 30) A spool that is shaped to fit the edge serves as one of the rollers for the belt. The belts used with this type must have the ability to stretch to conform to the spool. If the stretch available from a J weight belt is not enough, there are special bias weave belts available.

The *DeLappe sander* is an alternative to the spool and belt sander for small shops that don't want to invest in a large piece of equipment and yet need to sand a shaped edge in a limited production run. (Illus. 31)

To make a DeLappe sander, mount a disc of wood on a lathe face plate; shape the edge of the disc to the reverse image of the edge

that you need to sand. Cut a disc of J weight abrasive cloth. The disc should have a diameter large enough so that it can be folded over the shaped edge of the plywood disc. Cut radial slits into the disc leaving a central hub area uncut. Make two plywood flanges that will fit on either side of the shaped disc. Both flanges, the shaped disc and the abrasive cloth should have a hole in their exact center that will accept the threaded arbor shaft of the motor that will power the sander.

To assemble the sander place one flange on the shaft; next, place the abrasive cloth on the shaft and then the shaped disc. Fold the radially cut flaps of the abrasive cloth disc over the edge of the shaped disc. The flaps should all overlap each other so that the exposed edge will be the trailing edge when the sander is turning. Finally, place the other flange on the shaft and tighten the shaft nut to hold the assembly in place.

The DeLappe sander can be mounted directly to the motor shaft because any standard motor speed between 1200 RPM and 1800 RPM will work. Usually the motor shaft is mounted vertically extending through a table.

A DeLappe sander won't handle a large production run because of the small amount of abrasive exposed as opposed to a long belt; but for small runs it is an effective way to sand a shaped edge.

The *orbital sander* uses standard sheet sandpaper, usually one-half or one-third of a sheet, or specially made self-adhesive paper that is precut to the correct size and shape. The sandpaper clamps to the base of the machine. The sanding motion of an orbital sander is circular; the base travels in a small orbit. Older models of orbital sanders had a bad reputation because they left large, highly visible swirl marks on the work; but the new models have been greatly improved. The base travels much faster and in a smaller random orbit on new models so the swirl marks are barely visible. Of course, they are still there, so for the highest quality finish at least the final sanding should be done with a sander that has a straight line motion.

Orbital sanders don't cut as fast as belt sanders but they are light and easy to handle. They are especially useful for sanding joints where the grain direction changes because grain direction is not important when using an orbital sander. (Illus. 32)

Illus. 32. A modern orbital sander is capable of producing a very smooth surface free of discernible swirl marks. Orbital sanders are especially useful for sanding joints where the grain direction changes, because grain direction is unimportant with orbital sanding. This particular sander has a vacuum dust collection feature; the holes in the base collect the dust. Precut self-adhesive sandpaper makes changing paper easy.

Always start and stop an orbital sander with it lifted from the work; the base must be at full speed while in contact with the work to keep swirl marks to a minimum. For this reason, you should also avoid applying too much pressure to the sander as this will slow down the base. Move the sander in a back and forth motion with the direction of the grain. Remove any accumulations from the sandpaper as soon as they appear or they will cause swirl marks.

Oscillating sanders are similar to orbital sanders in general operation and appearance; but they have one major difference: the base oscillates back and forth in a straight-line motion rather than orbiting. For this reason, oscillating sanders are preferred for the final sanding operations. The only major disadvantage of oscillating sanders is that they cut slower than orbital sanders.

Drum sanders are useful for sanding edges. They use an abrasive coated cylindrical cardboard drum mounted on a rubber mandrel. Tightening a screw at one end of the mandrel expands the rubber, holding the drum in place. The drum can be mounted in a drill press or in a special machine. Some machines move the drum up and down as it rotates so the entire surface of the drum is utilized; this type is usually called a *spindle sander*. (Illus. 33) The drum sander is most useful for sanding curved edges because its cylindrical shape will follow the contours of the work. It's best to use the sander before assembling the pieces.

A *disc sander* consists of a backing disc to which a disc of coated abrasive is adhered. The disc is connected to the motor shaft. Stationary disc sanders have the disc mounted vertically and a horizontal table holds the work. Portable disc sanders use an angle drive to connect the disc to the motor; or in

Illus. 33. A spindle sander is especially adapted for sanding the inside edge of a circular cutout.

the case of very small versions, a shaft that fits into the chuck of a portable drill.

Disc sanders are used mostly for shaping rather than smoothing. The marks left by a disc sander are usually cross grain and semicircular. Portable disc sanders are likely to leave an irregular surface.

One of the most useful functions of a stationary disc sander is to sand the edge of a board that has been cut to shape with a band saw or a jig saw. A disc sander cuts very fast so you can use it to bring the board to its final shape, smoothing out any irregularities left by the sawing operation.

Portable disc sanders are used mostly for metal work, although they can perform some shaping operations in woodwork. They are not well suited for smoothing the surface of a board.

One unique type of disc sander that is useful in wood work is the *jointer sander*. This is a disc sander that mounts in place of the blade on a tilt arbor table saw. The disc is slightly thicker in the center than at the edges, making it a very squat cone. The tilt arbor of the saw should be set for a two degree angle; this compensates for the angle of the cone, so the sanding surface is square with the table. Because of its unique cone shape, the sanding marks left by the jointer sander are straight and parallel to the grain direction.

As its name implies, the jointer sander is used to produce a smooth square edge on a board. To use the sander, the table saw fence is set to the width of the board and the wood is fed through the machine similarly to the way it is when sawing to width. The amount of stock removed in one pass must be kept small, about $\frac{1}{32}$ in. This type of sander is an excellent way to remove mill marks from the edge of a board.

Flap sanders are made from flaps of cloth-backed abrasive that are connected to a central shaft; the shaft is usually mounted on a stationary grinder or in the chuck of an elec-

Illus. 34. Flap sanders will automatically conform to the surface of an irregularly shaped object.

Illus. 35. Die-cut flap sanders are used in production runs where the same shape will be sanded repeatedly.

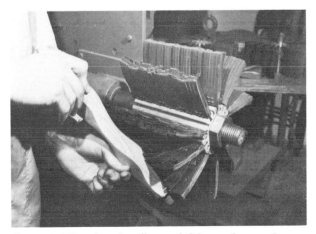

Illus. 36. The abrasive flaps of this sander can be replaced. They slide out of the slots in the central hub.

tric drill. Sometimes the flaps are slit into smaller sections and some types use brush bristles to hold the flap straight. (Illus. 34)

Flap sanders are most useful for sanding oddly shaped objects; for example, the concave interior of a carved bowl or the carved legs of French provincial furniture. Don't use a flap sander on intricately carved surfaces because it will flatten out the detail. Flap sanders are less aggressive than other types of power sanders. The scratch pattern produced by any given grade of flap sander will be about the same as the scratch pattern produced by a sanding belt that is one or two grades finer.

Flap sanders can be made of die-cut flaps that are pre-cut to a specific shape. This type is useful in production runs where the same shape will be sanded repeatedly. (Illus. 35)

Most flap sanders must be entirely replaced when the grit becomes dull or worn off, but some types have replaceable sections or they have a roll of abrasive cloth in the hub that can be rolled out to renew the cutting area. (Illus. 36)

In order for the flaps to best conform to the shape of the object, J weight cloth is usually used. For longer life and more aggressive cutting, X weight cloth is sometimes used. When X weight cloth is used it is usually slashed into strips for better conformability. The arbor speed of a flap wheel plays a role in its conformability, because centrifugal force makes the flap seem stiffer at faster speeds. Generally, flap wheels run at between 1200 RPM and 1800 RPM. Decreasing the speed increases the sander's ability to conform to the shape of the object, while increasing the speed will make the sander remove wood faster, but it won't conform to the shape as well, so some of the details will be flattened out.

Removing Dust. The final step in wood preparation is removing all of the accumulated dust from the surface and pores of the wood. Any dust left on the wood will show up in the final finish as small bumps. To remove the large quantities of dust left from sanding, a bristle brush works well; brush with the grain to get the dust out of the pores. (Illus. 38)

A vacuum cleaner fitted with a brush attachment is an excellent way of removing the dust. Compressed air can also be used to blow the dust from the wood, but it has several disadvantages. First, whenever you blow dust off it will be spread throughout the shop and will settle on other projects you are working on. This is especially bad if you use the same area to apply varnish or other finishes. Another disadvantage is that airborne dust poses a health hazard. *So, if you use compressed air to remove dust, do it in a well-ventilated area and use a low pressure setting.*

After most of the dust has been removed using one of the above methods, use a tack rag to get the last traces of dust off. A tack rag is a piece of cheesecloth that has been treated to make it attract dust. They aren't very expensive and can be purchased at any paint store. Rub the tack rag over the surface until

Illus. 37. Dust removal is vital to producing a smooth finish. A brush will reach into the pores of the wood to get out the dust that has accumulated there.

all of the dust has been removed. When one part of the tack rag becomes excessively coated with dust, unfold the rag and refold it so that a fresh surface is exposed.

Whitewood Inspection. Before any finish is applied to wood, it is said to be "in the white." Operations performed on the wood at this point are called whitewood operations. After all of the wood preparation steps are complete, you should perform a whitewood inspection to make sure they were all done correctly. Here is a quick review of the major steps in wood preparation:

1. Plane the surface to remove mill marks. Keep the blade sharp and set the plane iron cap $\frac{1}{32}$ in. away from the tip of the blade. Adjust the plane to take a very shallow cut.
2. Scrape the surface with a hand scraper or a cabinet scraper. Keep the blade sharp. It should produce fine shavings. If it produces dust, it needs to be resharpened.
3. Fill all nail holes and other defects. Sand the filler smooth with the surrounding surface.
4. Sand the surface with aluminum oxide sandpaper. Use a hardwood block initially to back up the sandpaper. Continue sanding with the first grade of sandpaper and the wood block until all high spots and scratches have been removed, then switch to a padded sanding block for all subsequent grades of sandpaper.
5. Remove all dust from the wood. Use a brush or vacuum to remove most of the dust, then wipe the surface with a tack rag to get the last traces of dust off.

When you perform your inspection, check to see that all of the above operations were performed satisfactorily. Check for any remaining mill marks or other surface defects. Look carefully at the results of the sanding operation. Are there any cross grain scratches? Is the surface smooth and free from fuzzy wood fibres? Are there any swirl marks left as a result of orbital sanding?

Check around glue joints to see if there is any remaining glue on the surface. Also examine nail holes and other areas that have been filled: are they all filled flush with the surface or has the putty shrunk and left a depressed surface? Is there any putty smeared around the hole? Has the putty been adequately sanded?

Any problems found in the whitewood inspection should be corrected before proceeding to other finishing steps. At this point they are easily remedied, but later they will become more noticeable and harder to correct as the finish is applied.

PREVIOUSLY FINISHED WOOD

When working with wood that has been previously finished, you must decide whether to attempt to repair and revitalize the existing finish or remove the finish and start over. This decision is based on two factors, the condition of the existing finish and whether or not the existing finish is aesthetically pleasing to you. If you like the present finish but it is dull and lifeless, the solution may simply be a good cleaning with a finish rejuvenator. Minor damages can easily be repaired, but major damage to the finish usually necessitates removal of the finish.

Cleaning, Restoring and Repairing the Finish

Cleaning and Rejuvenating Finishes.
When a finish looks dull and lifeless but is otherwise in good condition, you can usually bring it back to life by cleaning off the years of accumulated wax and grime. A product called wax and silicone remover or wax and grease remover contains special solvents that are well-suited for this job. Work in a well-ventilated area, because the fumes are flammable and toxic. Apply the solvent with a rag. Thoroughly wet a section of the finish with the solvent, then use a clean rag to buff

it dry. Refold the rag frequently to expose a clean surface, otherwise you will simply smear the deposits around instead of removing them. This type of solvent won't harm most finishes, so if the underlying finish is in good condition all that is needed is a coat of paste wax to bring out its beauty.

If the finish is still dull after cleaning, the top surface needs to be restored. You can polish it with pumice and rottenstone as described in Chapter 7 or you can use a finish restorer.

Finish restorers combine special solvents with tung oil to dissolve a thin layer of the old finish and replace it with tung oil. Most companies market several strength products. The first type contains a high concentration of tung oil and very few solvents. It is used almost like furniture polish to add a layer of oil without removing any of the old finish. The second type of product is usually referred to as a cleaner. It contains stronger solvents that dissolve the accumulated grime from the surface along with an extremely thin layer of the finish. As the cleaner is buffed off, a layer of tung oil is left on the surface. The third type is sometimes called a finish restorer or rejuvenator. It contains strong solvents similar to the type used in strippers. This product should only be used on finishes that are in need of major restoration. Before applying any product of this type, read the directions on the container thoroughly because application techniques can vary from one type to another.

Danish oil is another product that can be used to rejuvenate a finish. The type that contains a mixture of oils and solvents rather than pure tung oil is best for this application. First clean the finish with wax and silicone remover, then apply a thin coat of Danish oil with a rag and immediately buff it out with a dry rag. Start in an inconspicuous spot to make sure the oil is compatible with the existing finish.

The liquid wax that Danish oil manufacturers market for use with their finishes also makes a good finish rejuvenator. It contains solvents that clean the surface while you are applying the wax. It is available in colors to match the existing finish so it also hides small defects in the finish. Apply a wet coat with a rag and thoroughly clean the finish by rubbing vigorously while it is still wet. Wipe this coat off while it is still wet to remove the grime you have loosened, then apply a thin coat with a fresh rag and let it dry. Finally, use a dry cloth to buff the surface to the desired lustre.

Crazing. As a finish ages, it sometimes becomes brittle and many hairline cracks develop; this defect is called crazing. You can sometimes repair a crazed surface by applying a solvent to dissolve the finish and then letting it harden. This is an unpredictable process, so you should only attempt it if you are prepared to refinish the piece anyway if the process should fail.

Thoroughly clean the finish with a wax and silicone remover. If the old finish is shellac, use denatured alcohol as the solvent; if the finish is lacquer, use lacquer thinner. If the old finish is varnish or if you aren't sure of the finish used, buy a special solvent called amalgamator. Apply the solvent to the finish by spraying, padding, or brushing; spraying is best. Use enough solvent to completely wet the surface. The solvent will slowly dissolve the finish and the cracks will flow together. Let the finish dry as if it were a freshly applied top coat. If the process is successful, the finish will look like a new top coat has been applied. You can use steel wool or pumice and rottenstone to polish the surface to the desired lustre.

Scratches. Scratches are probably the most common type of damage that furniture receives. Most are minor and relatively easy to repair. If the scratch hasn't cut through the protective film of the top coat into the wood below, you can polish out the scratch. Use pumice to rub out the affected area until the scratch is removed, taking care not to rub clear through the finish. Then polish the area with rottenstone until it matches the surrounding finish. Complete directions for using pumice and rottenstone are given in Chapter 7. You can sometimes fill a minor scratch by rubbing a piece of walnut nutmeat or a block of beeswax over the scratch.

When the scratch is deep, it will cut through the finish and expose the bare wood below. This creates another problem, because the scratch will need to be stained to match the surrounding wood. How you handle a deep scratch depends on the location of the scratch. If it is in a highly visible area like a table top, you need to blend the scratch into the surrounding finish perfectly; but if it is in a less visible area like a chair leg, all you need to do is color the scratch approximately the same color as the surrounding finish. There are several simple ways to color a scratch. One way is to apply colored furniture polish to the scratch; several companies make a scratch hiding polish that is quite effective, especially on dark finishes. There are also specially made soft-tip markers available for the purpose of coloring scratches. The markers come in a variety of colors that will closely match almost any finish. You can even use ordinary permanent felt tip markers, if you can find the correct color. Use a very fine point and be careful to only color the damaged area; smearing the ink onto the undamaged finish will make the repaired area seem larger and call more attention to it. The wax filler sticks that were discussed previously are also useful for coloring minor scratches; but because they always remain soft, they should not be used on areas that will receive a lot of wear.

When the scratch must blend into the surrounding finish perfectly, there is really only one method that will produce satisfactory results. First you must stain the wood to match the rest of the finish. Spot-finishing stains come as a powder; they are soluble in alcohol or lacquer. Analyze the existing finish to determine whether a penetrating stain or a shading stain was used. If a penetrating stain was used, dissolve a small amount of the spot-finishing stain in alcohol and apply it with a small artist's brush to the scratch. Try to confine the stain to the scratch; this type of stain will soak through most finishes, so if you get some outside of the scratch, it is hard to remove. Refer to Chapter 5 for a complete discussion of color mixing. Next, fill the scratch with spot-finishing lacquer using a small artist's brush. Spot-finishing lacquer is a special type of lacquer that is compatible with most finishes. If a shading stain was used in the original finish, dissolve the powdered stain into some of the spot-finishing lacquer and use a small brush to fill the scratch. When the lacquer has dried, use 600 grit wet-or-dry sandpaper to sand the lacquer level with the surrounding surface; then polish the area to the correct lustre with pumice and rottenstone.

Water Marks.   Finishes vary in their resistance to water; when water is left on the surface of a finish that is not water resistant, a white discoloration occurs. This is called blushing. Usually the water hasn't soaked all

Illus. 38. Water marks can usually be removed by wiping over them with a pad that has been moistened with alcohol.

the way through the finish and in these cases it is easy to remove. Make a small pad by covering a ball of wool or cotton with a piece of close-weave cotton or linen fabric. Wet the pad with denatured alcohol until it is just barely damp. Wipe the pad over the water mark in long, straight strokes with the grain. Keep the pad in constant motion and lift it from the surface after each stroke. (Illus. 37) The alcohol has an attraction for water, and it will draw the water out of the finish. Keep padding over the area until the mark disappears, unless the finish begins to soften; in that case, let the finish dry for an hour or so and repeat the padding until the mark is gone.

If alcohol won't remove the mark, try rubbing the area with pumice and rottenstone.

If the water has been standing on the wood for a long time, as happens when a houseplant pot is placed directly on a table, the water will soak clear through the finish and discolor the wood below or raise the grain. In that case, you will have to sand the finish off of the affected area and start over again. If the area is large, it is best to strip the piece and refinish; but if it is not too large, sand down the area until all of the stain is removed, then spot finish the area using the directions given for worn spots. Sometimes the discoloration will soak so deep into the wood that it is impractical to sand it out; in that case, use one of the bleaches described on pages 49-50 to bleach out the stain.

Worn Spots.   The finish on corners, edges and other areas that receive a lot of handling frequently wears off before the rest of the finish. (Illus. 38) You can spot finish these areas to match the original finish. The most important factor in achieving a good result is your ability to match the original color. Spot-finishing stains come in a large variety of colors, and you can mix them to achieve any shade desired. Refer to Chapter 5 for directions on mixing colors. Experiment on a

Illus. 39. Edges and corners receive more wear than other areas, so the finish is more likely to wear off them first. This chair arm has a considerable amount of visible wear.

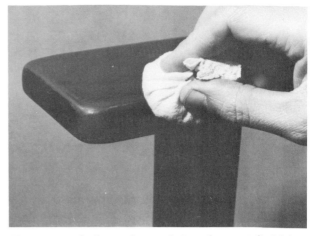

Illus. 41. Rub the pad containing the spot-finishing stain over the worn areas in long, even strokes, with the grain. When the color is correct, protect the stain with clear spot-finishing lacquer.

Illus. 40. To repair the worn finish, moisten a pad with spot-finishing lacquer, then dip it into some dry powder spot-finishing stain. Work the stain into the pad until it is blended with the lacquer.

piece of scrap wood of the same species until you are satisfied with the color. To begin, make a French polishing pad as described in Chapter 4. Moisten the pad with spot-finishing lacquer (also called padding lacquer). Next dip the pad into the correct color powdered spot-finishing stain. (Illus. 39) If you need to mix colors, you can dip the pad into more than one color or you can apply the different colors in separate coats. Work the pad over a piece of scrap to evenly distribute the stain in the pad, then pad the stain onto the wood. Rub the pad over the wood in long rapid strokes with the grain. Don't stop the pad while it is touching the wood. Keep padding over the area, adding more stain and lacquer to the pad as necessary, until you are satisfied with the color. (Illus. 40) After the stain is applied, let it dry; then switch to a clean pad. Moisten this pad with clear spot-finishing lacquer and apply several coats to the area to build up a protective coating over the stain. After the lacquer is dry, buff it with 4/0 steel wool or polish it with pumice and rottenstone to give it the desired lustre. The film produced by padding is thin, so take care not to rub through the finish.

Dents, Gouges, and Burns

Dents, gouges, and burns all leave a hole that is lower than the surrounding surface. Before any finishing can be done, the hole must be filled. Sometimes dents can be repaired without filling, because a dent still has the same amount of wood fibres as the surrounding wood; they are just compressed. If you can get the fibres to swell back to their original shape, the dent will disappear. The simplest way to make the fibres swell is to apply water to the dent. If the water hasn't removed the dent after several applications, thoroughly wet the area, then heat it. A hair blowdryer is a good way to heat the wood without damaging it. You can also try a clothes iron, if you protect the wood with a damp cloth. (Illus. 42) If the dent still hasn't completely come back to its original shape, try placing an ice cube on it while it is still hot. If all of these methods fail, the area will have to be filled.

There are two ways to fill dents, gouges, and burns: wood putty and burn-in sticks. Before using either type, clean out the hole with a knife blade or carving gouge to remove any charred wood or loose splinters. If you slightly undercut the edges of the hole, the patch will stay in place better.

Wood putty comes in two basic types: solvent based and water based. Solvent-based putty tends to shrink as it dries, so you must build it up higher than the surface to allow for shrinkage. The water-based type doesn't shrink, so you can apply it level with the surface. You can mix dry powdered stain with the water-based putty to match the color of the putty to the surrounding stain. The solvent-based putty is available in several colors, so you can pick one that is close to the correct color.

Before applying the putty, use a small cotton swab or a brush to apply a small amount of glue to the inside of the hole. This will help the patch stay in place longer. Use a small putty knife or a screwdriver blade to fill the hole with putty. The blade should be small enough so that you don't smear too much putty on the surrounding finish. For small holes a screwdriver is better than a putty knife.

Once the putty is dry, use a very small piece of sandpaper to sand it flush with the surrounding surface. Avoid scratching the surrounding finish with the sandpaper.

Use the methods described for repairing worn spots to stain and finish the patch.

When the surrounding wood doesn't have

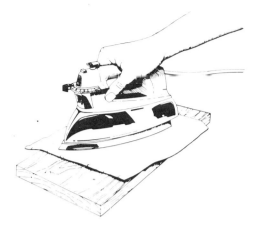

Illus. 42. An iron can be used to steam out dents. Protect the wood surface with a damp cloth.

a prominent grain pattern, it is only necessary to match the color of the patch to the wood; but if the wood has a prominent grain that passes through the patch area, you will need to duplicate the grain pattern in the patched area. First color the patch the same color as the lightest part of the grain. Then dip an artist's brush into a little spot finishing stain mixed with lacquer that is the color of the dark lines of the grain. Use the brush to connect the grain lines that are interrupted by the patch. Artist's oil paints or acrylics can also be used for this operation.

Burn-in sticks are made of solid lacquer or shellac. They come in a wide variety of colors and can be mixed to match any finish. (Illus. 42) They have several advantages over wood putty. First, they don't shrink; second, they are applied hot and harden as they cool, so you don't have to wait for them to dry; finally, if they are carefully color matched to the finish, they form a complete repair with no additional finishing necessary. Burn-in sticks are the choice of most professional spot finishers.

Burn-in sticks are applied with a special knife called a burn-in knife. (Illus. 43) The knife must be heated to melt the sticks. Electric burn-in knives are available; they operate

Illus. 43. Burn-in sticks come in a wide selection of colors.

Illus. 44. A burn-in knife resembles a kitchen spatula with a bend at the end. It is much thicker than an ordinary spatula, so it will retain heat longer.

like a soldering iron. An ordinary burn-in knife looks like a spatula; it is heated with a propane torch or other heat source. (Illus. 44) As you work with the hot knife, take care not to burn the surrounding undamaged finish; some suppliers of burn-in sticks also sell a protective balm that is smeared onto the surrounding finish to help prevent damage.

To fill a hole with a burn-in stick, heat the knife, occasionally removing it from the flame and testing the temperature by pressing a burn-in stick against the blade; the knife is ready when it melts the stick, but it's too hot if the stick burns or bubbles. Press the end of the knife against the edge of the stick, and slice off a thin slab of the stick. Let the slab sit on the knife for a moment until it is completely melted, then press it into the hole. (Illus. 45) Use the tip of the knife to smooth and level the patch. In a few minutes, the patch will cool and harden. When it is hard, finish the job of smoothing the patch with sandpaper or special cutting fluid. The manufacturers of some types of burn-in sticks also make a special cutting fluid that will dissolve the patch but won't hurt the surrounding wood. Apply a small amount of the fluid to a stiff pad and rub over the patch as if you were sanding. The fluid will smooth out the patch, but the surrounding finish will be unaffected. You can also use 600 grit wet-or-dry sandpaper to smooth the patch; lubri-

Illus. 45. A propane torch can be used to heat the knife. The knife should be removed from the heat every few seconds to check its temperature by pressing it against a burn-in stick. If the knife causes the stick to burn or bubble, it is too hot.

Illus. 46. Use the burn-in knife to press the melted material into the hole.

cate the paper with a little water and carefully sand the patch. Try not to sand the surrounding finish. If you are satisfied with the way the patch looks, use pumice and rottenstone to polish the patch to the proper lustre. No additional finish is needed. If you want to change the color of the patch or if you need to paint in grain lines, use spot finishing stains and lacquer.

You can mix two or more colors of burn-in sticks to make a custom color. To mix the sticks, scrape a little of each stick onto the hot knife; use another hot knife to blend the colors together by mixing them back and forth. If the mixture hardens before you are able to apply it, heat the second knife again and use it to remove the mixture from the first knife, and apply it to the hole.

Solvent and Steel Wool Refinishers. When the existing finish is beyond the help of a finish restorer but not so severely damaged to warrant its complete removal, a solvent and steel wool refinisher is a good choice. This method removes the top layers of the old finish but leaves the underlying stain and filler intact. This method is very useful for removing darkened varnish or for lightening a dark finish to meet modern tastes.

To use it you put some solvent (lacquer thinner for most finishes, alcohol for shellac) in a shallow dish. Dip a fine (at least 4/0) steel wool pad into the solvent and rub it over a small section of the finish to be removed. (Illus. 47) The solvent will dissolve the old top coat and the particles of finish will lodge in the steel wool; dip the steel wool into the solvent again and rinse out the pad. Work in small sections at a time and replace the solvent when it becomes thick with old finish. When the desired effect is achieved, use a clean steel wool pad and a small amount of clean solvent to clean up the surface by rubbing in long strokes with the grain along the entire length of the board.

Because the fine steel wool won't produce

Illus. 47. The solvent and steel wool method of removing an old finish leaves the wood ready for the application of a new top coat without any further preparation. Because this old drawer was finished with a lacquer shading stain, the stripped surface is considerably lighter than the old finish. If the drawer had been stained with an aniline stain and finished with a clear top coat, the stripped surface would have been approximately the same color as the old finish.

deep scratches in the wood, no further sanding is required. If the finish you are removing is a colored top coat such as a shading lacquer or a varnish stain, the color of the wood after stripping will be much lighter. If the old finish is a clear top coat over stain, the color will remain about the same because only the top coat will be removed. If you're happy with the color left after the top coat has been removed, no staining is required. If you prefer a lighter color, additional rubbing with the solvent will lighten the color. If you want to darken or change the color, you can apply an oil stain. Any type top coat can be applied. Many people prefer to use an oil finish after this type of refinisher is used because it is easy to apply and it uniformly gives good results.

There are several brand-name refinishers of this type on the market and all of them produce good results; however, you can save a lot of money by using lacquer thinner instead of a brand-name refinisher. In most cases ordinary lacquer thinner will work just as well as the brand-name products, and yet it costs one-third to one-fourth as much. For really tough finishes, you may have to use one of the brand-name products; they contain methylene chloride while lacquer thinner doesn't, but lacquer thinner will dissolve most conventional finishes. If the old finish is shellac, denatured alcohol can be used as the solvent. This type of refinishing is not recommended for synthetic finishes like epoxy or polyurethane. This method also should not be used on painted surfaces.

Note: Wear neoprene gloves when using this method, because the solvents will dry out your skin and cause irritation. Laquer thinner and alcohol are flammable, so work in a well-ventilated area away from pilot lights or other sources of ignition.

Here are step-by-step directions for the solvent and steel wool method:

1. Pour some solvent into a shallow dish. Wear neoprene gloves. Dip fine steel wool pad into solvent. Squeeze pad to remove excess. Rub pad in a circular motion over a small area (approximately 12 in. diameter).

2. Return the pad to the solvent dish to rinse out the accumulated residue of the old finish. When the area you are working on is cleaned of the old finish, move to another section. You can stop the process at any time to return later without fear of lap marks.

When the solvent becomes thick with residue, replace it. You may need to replace the steel wool also, if the project is large.

3. When the entire surface has been cleaned of the old finish, replace the steel wool with a clean pad and fill the dish with clean solvent. Dip the pad into the solvent and squeeze it fairly dry. Rub the pad with the grain to remove the circular marks left by the previous operation. Finish with long strokes running the entire length of the board to produce the most even effect.

Let the surface dry at least half an hour (much more if the humidity is high) before proceeding with additional finishing steps.

Removing the Finish

When the existing finish has deteriorated to the point that repair and restoration techniques are inadequate, then the finish must be removed. More frequently though, the finish is removed because the existing finish is no longer in line with current taste in color or appearance. In either case the procedure is the same.

There are several methods of removing the old finish but they can be divided into two major categories: mechanical and chemical.

Mechanical Methods. The mechanical methods involve more physical labor than the other methods, but they have two major advantages: they don't leave any residual chemicals on the wood and they won't raise the grain of the wood. All of the mechanical methods are best suited for flat surfaces, because it is very difficult to use them to get into small details.

A *scraper* can be used to mechanically remove some finishes. They work best on brittle finishes. Scraping is best suited for flat areas but there are small scrapers that are shaped to fit mouldings and other details. When using a scraper, you need to take care that the scraper doesn't gouge into the wood. Because soft woods are so easily gouged, scraping is better suited for hard woods.

Sanding is another mechanical method of removing the old finish. Use open coat sandpaper or sandpaper with a nonclog coating. The sanding technique is similar to the technique used on new wood, except you need to clean the sandpaper more often. A wire brush is useful for removing the accumulations of old finish from the sandpaper. To remove the finish, you can start with a very coarse grade of sandpaper such as 50 grit, but switch to a finer grade as soon as you break through to bare wood. Power sanders will speed up the operation. Don't use an orbital sander (p. 35) with 50 grit paper because the resulting swirl marks will be very difficult to remove. A belt sander (p. 22) is more appropriate because the sanding action is in line with the grain, but be careful not to damage the wood by holding the sander unevenly or staying in one place too long. Once the finish has been removed, complete the sanding operation as if you were working with new wood. If the piece you are working on has been veneered or is made of plywood, it may not be possible to completely sand off all of the stain without sanding through the veneer. In that case, you will have to use a chemical bleach if you want to completely remove the stain. However, this is usually only necessary when the new finish will be considerably lighter than the old one.

Heat is another mechanical means of removing the old finish. Most finishes can be softened with heat and easily scraped from the surface. Heat can loosen glue joints, especially on older furniture, and it may cause veneers to buckle or come loose.

A propane torch is frequently recommended for this; but, because it can easily scorch the wood, a torch should only be used for exterior surfaces that won't receive a fine finish. Their use indoors is not recommended because of the likelihood of fire. Also, flame should be kept far from glass. Usually a special torch tip is used that spreads the flame over a wider area. Aim the tip of the flame at the surface and rapidly move it back and forth over a small area. As soon as the finish begins to wrinkle or takes on a shiny appearance, remove the flame and quickly scrape the area with a scraper. You must work fast because the finish will reharden as it cools.

Interior work and furniture should not be stripped with a torch. For these applications use either a *heat gun* (Illus. 48) or a *heat plate* (Illus. 49). The heat gun is the best because it can be used on mouldings and turned elements. It looks like a hair dryer but it produces a much hotter stream of air. *Caution:* The air stream from a heat gun will burn your skin. Don't use near glass. Direct the

hot air at a small section of finish until the finish wrinkles or changes appearance. Quickly remove the finish with a putty knife or scraper.

A heat plate resembles an electric range burner but the heating element faces down

Illus. 48. The heat gun is a heavy-duty industrial product that, despite its relatively high initial cost, saves money on big jobs because of the escalating cost of chemical strippers. It works best on thick layers of paint and does not vaporize the lead in old lead-based paint. It is too slow for most exterior work.

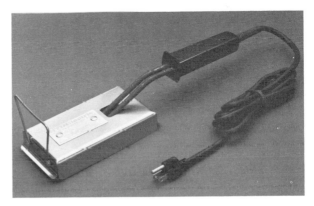

Illus. 49. The heat plate can be used on clapboard siding and other large, flat surfaces such as large panels, shingles and doors. The wire frame makes it possible to put it down without turning the unit off. A shield reflects the heat onto the paint.

instead of up. Some types have small legs to keep the element off the surface; others must be held above the surface being stripped. Because the heat plate uses radiant heat rather than hot air as the heat gun does, it is much easier to scorch the surface, so take care and watch the surface closely. As soon as the finish appears soft, remove the heat plate and scrape the area.

Chemical Strippers. When it is necessary to remove the previous finish entirely, chemical strippers are probably the easiest method. However they do have disadvantages; some types will raise the grain or may loosen veneers or glue joints, and they contain potentially hazardous chemicals and solvents. When using chemical strippers, be prepared for the mess and disposal problems involved. Work in a well-ventilated area, protect surrounding surfaces from stray globs of finish and stripper and protect yourself with neoprene gloves, goggles and protective clothing. Also make certain that no flames (cigarettes, pilot lights, etc.) are nearby.

Before the advent of modern strippers, caustic solutions such as lye were used extensively to remove old varnish or paint. The problem with caustic removers is that they are difficult to completely neutralize or remove, so they create problems in the new finish, can darken woods high in tannin (such as oak), and they pose safety and health hazards for the user.

Modern strippers use a combination of solvents and chemicals to soften the old finish. When choosing a stripper it pays to use the best quality. You can tell a quality stripper by the fact that it contains methylene chloride.

Inexpensive strippers that don't contain methylene chloride use a combination of solvents to soften the finish; because these solvents evaporate very quickly, the stripper usually also contains paraffin to slow down the evaporation. These type strippers are

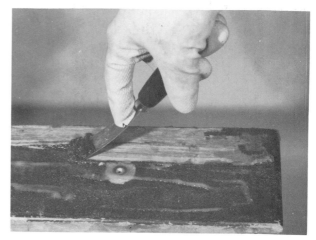

Illus. 50. After the stripper has loosened the old finish, a putty knife can be used to lift the finish off.

rather messy to use; you have to physically loosen the softened finish from the wood by scraping or with steel wool. After the finish has been removed, you have to carefully wash the wood with alcohol, paint thinner, or mineral spirits to remove all traces of the paraffin left by the stripper. If any paraffin remains on the wood, it will later cause problems in the new finish.

Strippers containing methylene chloride are by far the best and have the advantage of being non-flammable. They penetrate the finish and loosen its bond to the wood; the finish will wrinkle and blister, making it easy to remove. The blisters become larger as the stripper continues to loosen the bond. Eventually you can use a wide blade putty knife to lift off the old finish film in large sheets. (Illus. 49) Most removers of this type don't require any rinsing. The strength of this type of stripper depends on the amount of methylene chloride it contains. For ordinary varnish, lacquer or shellac, you don't need the strength of the strippers with the highest amounts of methylene chloride; so you can save money by using a stripper with a lower concentration. For synthetic finishes such as epoxy, alkyds, or polyurethane, you will need to use a stripper with the highest concentration of methylene chloride. Remember

48

to provide for ventilation since it can seriously irritate the lungs and even the heart.

Strippers come in liquid, semi-paste, and paste form. Liquid stripper is most useful for flat surfaces where it won't run off. Semi-paste and paste strippers contain an ingredient to make them gel; they will stick to vertical surfaces better than liquid.

Note: When using a stripper, follow the directions on the container and observe all of the safety warnings. It's important to wear goggles and neoprene gloves, be certain that there is adequate ventilation and avoid all heat sources such as lighted cigarettes and pilot lights.

Commercial stripping companies. Do-it-yourself stripping is fine if you are willing to invest the time and work necessary to do it. If your main concern is saving money, then do-it-yourself stripping is the best way to go. If you're willing to spend a little more money, you should consider having the stripping done professionally. It is especially advisable for intricate pieces such as chairs. The cost of having a commercial stripper remove the old finish is usually quite reasonable, so it's a good idea to call for a quote before stripping something yourself.

Commercial strippers use two different methods of removing the finish; the older method uses a hot dip tank filled with caustic chemicals. This method can loosen glue joints, darken oak, and substantially raise the grain. The other and preferred method is called the flow over method or cold tank. This method of commercial stripping won't loosen glue joints and only slightly raises the grain. In the flow over method the furniture is placed in a dry tank. Solvent-type stripper is pumped by a recirculating pump through a filter and out a hose that flows the stripper over the piece of furniture.

Wood that has been dip-stripped should be air-dried for at least three weeks before refinishing or warping could result.

Bleaching. Bleaching is a process that removes most of the natural color from wood. It is usually used when the desired finish is lighter than the natural color of the wood. It is also used when two pieces of wood to be used in the same project vary a great deal in color. Bleaching the darker board will make it match the lighter one better. Light-colored wood that is left unfinished for a long time will darken and eventually take on a grey look, especially if it is exposed to the weather. Bleach will restore the wood to its original light color.

Note: Bleaches contain harsh chemicals so wear neoprene or rubber gloves and goggles.

Bleaching will raise the grain, so you will have to sand the surface after the bleaching process.

Ordinary household liquid chlorine bleach will work for some bleaching operations. Apply the bleach straight from the bottle. Let the bleach dry and apply another coat if necessary. When the desired effect is achieved, rinse the wood thoroughly with water.

For maximum effect, a commercial wood bleach is recommended. Bleaches made specifically for wood are much stronger than household bleach. They usually consist of two parts that must be mixed just before use. Follow directions on the container for rinsing and neutralizing.

Oxalic acid was extensively used as a bleach before the two-part bleaches were developed. It isn't as strong as the new bleaches and it is hard to get an even color when bleaching large areas, but some people still prefer it to the newer bleaches. One reason is that the wood retains more of its original character.

Oxalic acid comes as dry crystals; to use as a bleach the crystals must be mixed with hot water. Apply the acid with a nylon brush. When the desired amount of bleaching has taken place, the area must be washed with water. The last step is neutralizing the acid by washing the area with a solution of three ounces of borax mixed with one gallon of water.

After stripping off an old finish, some traces of stain may remain on the wood. Sometimes you can bleach out the stain; it depends on what type of stain was originally used.

There are commercial stain removers that perform very well. The stain removers are formulated to work on specific types of stains. One type removes aniline stains; another type removes oil stains; and a third type removes other miscellaneous types of stains. Most commercially made furniture is stained with aniline stain, so the aniline stain remover is the type to try if you are refinishing a factory-made piece.

2 · Finishing Tools

Before applying any finishing material, you need to decide which finishing tools to use. There are several general types of tools for applying a finish; each has a place in the finishing process. The three most common types of finishing tools are brushes, pad applicators, and spray equipment. The tools you choose will play an important role in how the completed finish looks and the amount of labor involved in applying the finish, so you need to pick the tool that best fits the job at hand.

BRUSHES

Brushes are the oldest type of finishing tools, dating back to ancient Egypt. Today they are still the tool of choice for many finishing operations, although spraying has taken over as the leader for applying the top coats of a finish.

Brushes consist of a set of filaments attached to a handle by means of a ferrule. The filaments are attached to the ferrule with a setting compound. Vulcanized rubber was once the most popular setting compound, but epoxy resin has now taken the lead. The filaments are separated into groups in the ferrule by tapered plugs called fillers. The ferrule is attached to the handle with nails or rivets. (Illus. 51)

Brushes are categorized by the type of filament used. Two general categories are natural and synthetic filaments. Solvent-based products such as lacquer, shellac, and spirit stain are usually applied with a brush that contains natural filaments. Water-based products should be applied with a synthetic filament brush. Oil-based products such as varnish, oil stain, or oil paint can be applied with either natural or synthetic filaments.

Natural Brushes

The term bristle has acquired several meanings; to most people it means the filaments in any type of brush. Technically the

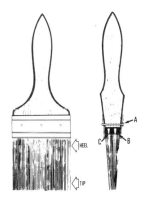

Illus. 51. Parts of a brush: (A) rivet, (B) setting compound, (C) filler.

term bristle can be applied only to the hair of the Chinese hog, but many people refer to any natural filament brush as a bristle brush. Besides bristle there are many other natural filaments used in brushes; some are very expensive and are used for specialty brushes such as sign painting, pin striping, and artists' brushes, while others are inexpensive and are used as a substitute for bristle in inexpensive brushes.

Red sable is used for high quality artists' and lettering brushes. It is obtained from the Siberian mink.

Black sable is also used for artists' and lettering brushes as well as striping brushes. It comes from the Central American civet cat.

Camel hair is used mostly for watercolor brushes and striping brushes. It doesn't come from a camel at all; it comes from the tails of Russian and Siberian squirrels.

Ox hair is used alone for striping and sign painters' brushes. It is blended with China bristle to make high quality general-purpose brushes. It is obtained from the ears of cattle.

Horsehair is one of the filaments used as a substitute for bristle in inexpensive brushes. It doesn't perform as well as bristle and so it should be avoided when the highest quality work is to be done.

Palmetto comes from the palmetto tree and is also used as a substitute for bristle.

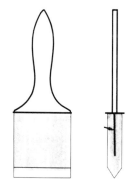

Illus. 52. Foam brush construction. Notice the plastic stiffener that extends through the center of the foam. Without this stiffener, the brush would be too limp to use effectively.

Tampico is another filament used as a substitute for bristle. It comes from cactus. Because it is resistant to chemicals, it is used in brushes for applying chemical stains and bleaches.

Synthetic Brushes

Since the 1940's, manmade materials have become increasingly popular as a brush material. When it is made properly, a synthetic filament brush can equal or surpass the performance of a natural filament brush. Synthetic filaments are better suited for use with water-based materials than natural filaments. Natural filaments lose their resiliency and become limp in water while synthetics remain firm and springy. Some synthetics are affected by the solvents found in lacquer or shellac, but the highest quality synthetics are not adversely affected and can be used with virtually any finishing material.

Nylon and polyester are the two most common synthetics used in brush manufacture; both make excellent brushes when the highest grade material is used. Styrene and polypropylene are sometimes used for inexpensive brushes, but their performance is not as good as nylon or polyester.

Foam brushes Another type of synthetic brush doesn't use filaments at all; instead a plastic foam is used. (Illus. 52) This type of brush can be very useful for applying stain because it applies a very even coat free of brush marks. (Illus. 53) Foam brushes can also be used successfully to apply varnish, but they tend to dissolve in lacquer and shellac.

Choosing a Brush

Choosing a brush can sometimes be a very confusing experience because of the wide range of types and prices available. Before attempting to select a brush, analyze what use you will put it to. For example, if you intend to use the brush to apply paint strip-

Illus. 53. Foam brushes are very good for applying stain. In this comparison between a foam brush and an inexpensive nylon brush, notice that the foam brush carries more stain and leaves a smooth application of stain without brush marks.

Illus. 54. Types of filaments: (A) straight, (B) tapered, (C) tapered and flagged.

per, it would be foolish to purchase a high quality brush since an inexpensive throw-away brush will do the job. On the other hand, to apply the final coat of varnish to a table top requires a very good brush.

The first step in choosing a brush is to decide on the type of filament. If you are using a water-based material, choose a synthetic filament. Nylon or polyester are best. Synthetics also work well with other finishing material besides water-based, so don't rule them out if you aren't using a water-based material. For general work the best natural brushes use a blend of ox hair and China bristle. The highest quality brushes will contain about 20 percent ox hair and 80 percent bristle by weight. Lower quality brushes will contain fewer ox hairs. The lowest quality natural brushes will substitute horsehair for the ox hair.

After deciding on the type of filament, examine the individual filaments in the brush. A high quality filament, whether natural or synthetic should possess the following characteristics (Illus. 54):

Taper The filament should be thicker at the end that attaches to the ferrule than it is at the tip.

Flagging The ends of the filament should be split. This allows the brush to carry more material and contributes to a smooth finish.

Spring The filaments should be resilient without being stiff. Press the brush against the back of your hand to feel the spring of the brush. The brush should bend easily without poking into your skin, and yet it should immediately spring back to its original shape when lifted away from your hand.

Length The filament should be approximately 50 percent longer than the width of the brush. This means that a two-inch brush should have filaments about three inches long.

When you have decided that the filaments are appropriate for the use you will put them to, check out the general construction of the brush. Filler strips in the ferrule divide the filaments into groups; this allows the brush to carry more material, if it is done correctly. Usually two filler strips are used. Quality brushes use thin filler strips. Inexpensive brushes sometimes use wide strips to cut down on the amount of filaments needed to fill the ferrule. However, if the filaments used are very inexpensive, there may not be any filler strips at all. Brush the filaments

53

across your hand several times to check for loose filaments. Any new brush will lose a few filaments at first, but excessive filament loss indicates that the setting compound is not adequate.

The shape of the handle is a matter of personal preference. Hold the handle in your hand and see if it fits comfortably and will give you adequate control. A flat or beaver tail handle is generally more comfortable for use on large surfaces, while a round handle is preferable for varnishing because it gives you more control. Handles can be made of wood or plastic; there is really no difference in the performance, so just because a brush has a wood handle it is not necessarily a better brush. Wood handles come either bare or with a finish applied. Although the finished handles may look nicer, they are a nuisance, if you intend to reuse the brush for a long time. The finish will tend to crack and flake off after exposure to the solvents used in the finishing materials and brush cleaners.

Brush Use and Care

In order to achieve the best possible results from a brush, it must be used and cared for properly. A brush should be held with the handle resting between your thumb and first finger. The flat part of the handle just above the ferrule should be grasped by the thumb on one side and the remaining fingers on the other. (Illus. 55) Dip the brush into the finishing material so that about one half of the filament length is submerged in the liquid. Don't dunk the brush in clear up to the ferrule. This is not only messy to work with, it will shorten the life of the brush by deteriorating the setting compound and causing accumulations of the finish to harden inside the ferrule.

As you withdraw the brush from the liquid, gently squeeze the excess from the brush by pressing it against the inside of the container. Don't rub the brush across the lip

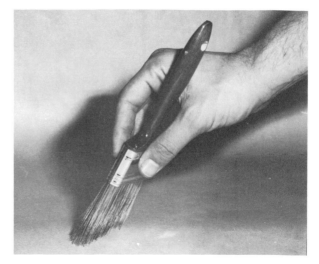

Illus. 55. Holding the brush in this manner gives you more control.

of the container as this will lead to a condition called fingering, where the filaments separate into bunches like several fingers.

The technique of applying the material to the wood depends on what type of finishing product you are using. Stains should be applied in long even strokes starting at one edge and continuing to the other, always following the grain direction. When applying top coats, start in the center of the board and work the finish towards each edge. This technique prevents the drips that occur if a full brush is used across an edge.

Fast-drying products like shellac or lacquer must be brushed out quickly, and once it has been applied it should not be brushed over again. Slower-drying products like varnish should first be flowed on. This means that a very full brush is used and the material is applied quite heavily. Then as soon as the surface is covered, brush over the surface again without applying any more material. This brushing-out process will smooth and even the coating.

A quality brush can give years of service if it is cared for properly. Always clean the brush with the same solvent used to thin the material you applied with the brush. It is generally a good idea to keep a separate brush for each type of material you use, since some materials are not compatible and traces of the old material in the brush may affect the new finish.

A *brush keeper* is a useful item if you use your brushes frequently. It is an airtight container with a rack to hang the brushes inside. (Illus. 56) A small amount of a special solvent is put in the bottom of the container. The brushes don't actually touch the solvent; the vapor from the solvent is what keeps the brush soft. With a brush keeper you can put a brush away, that will be used again in a day or two, after only a quick rinse out in solvent. The keeper will prevent the remaining finish from hardening in the brush. If you use this method, be sure to use the brush only with the same type of material unless you give it a thorough cleaning.

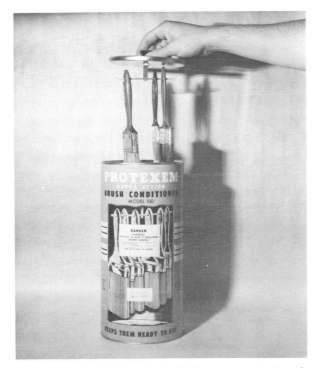

Illus. 56. A brush keeper will let you put a brush away with only minimal cleaning. Notice that the brushes are suspended from a rack by the hole in the handle. The end of the brush doesn't touch the bottom of the container.

If you will be storing the brush for longer than a few days, you must give it a complete cleaning. First rinse it in the proper solvent to remove as much of the finishing material as possible, then wash it with soap and running water to remove the last traces of finish and solvent. When you wash the brush, don't scrub the filaments back and forth as this will lead to fingering; instead, work the soap into a lather by rubbing along the length of the brush starting at the ferrule and working towards the tip. When the brush is clean, mould it into its original shape and hang it up to dry. Hanging a brush from its hole in the handle will ensure that the brush will dry in the correct shape. Never store a brush with its weight resting on the filaments, because the filaments will be permanently bent. The common practice of leaving a brush overnight resting on its filaments in a can of thinner is a sure way to ruin a brush.

A *brush comb* is a useful tool for cleaning a brush. It has widely spaced metal teeth that separate the filaments of a brush. (Illus. 57) It can be used to loosen the finish when you are rinsing the brush in solvent. It is also useful when you are trying to recover a brush that was improperly cleaned and has hardened deposits of finish, gluing the filaments into clumps.

A brush that has a large amount of hardened finish can be reclaimed in some cases, depending on what the finish is. Super-hard synthetic finishes like epoxy and polyurethane generally cannot be removed from the brush once they have cured, and the brush must be discarded. Varnish, shellac, and lacquer can usually be successfully removed by suspending the brush in a sealed container of lacquer thinner. Hang the brush by its handle so it won't rest on the bottom of the container. You may have to leave the brush in the thinner for several days to completely soften the hardened finish. There are also commercially made brush cleaners that will soften hardened brushes.

PAD APPLICATORS

Pad applicators are probably the best method of applying stain evenly. A pad applicator consists of a rectangular section of fabric that has thousands of short filaments attached, making it look like short-napped carpet. The fabric is bonded to a foam backing that is attached to a metal or plastic base. A handle is attached to the back of the base. (Illus. 58)

Pad applicators have many applications in house painting, but for wood finishing they are most useful as stain applicators. Almost any type of stain can be applied with a pad applicator, but spirit stains may dissolve the foam backing of some types so test a corner of the pad in spirit stain to see if it dissolves.

The foam backing holds a large amount of stain so you can cover a large area without refilling the applicator.

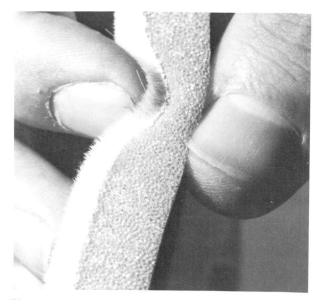

Illus. 58. The secret of the pad applicator's ability to hold more material is the foam backing. It acts like a sponge to hold liquid and gradually release it as needed. The carpetlike fabric applies the material to the work like a brush.

Illus. 57. A brush comb is a useful tool to help clean all of the finishing material from a brush. The widely spaced metal teeth separate the filaments of the brush to promote more thorough cleaning.

The pad applicator will apply the stain very uniformly; this is especially useful when it is desirable to apply the stain without further wiping to even out the coverage.

To use the applicator, pour a small amount of stain into a paint roller tray. The level of the stain in the tray should be low enough so that you can set the applicator in the tray and not completely submerge it. Fill the applicator by placing it in the tray and pressing it against the bottom of the tray to compress the foam. This will completely soak the foam with stain. Wipe the pad across the slanted part of the tray to remove the excess stain from the filaments.

Apply the stain to the wood in long even strokes with the grain. When the pad is full, apply only moderate pressure and increase the pressure gradually as the stain is used up to keep the amount applied uniform. Tilting the applicator slightly so that more pressure is applied to the rear edge will produce the same uniform appearance as wiping the stain after application. This is because the

Illus. 59. Pad applicators are well suited for applying stain. Wiping stain can be applied and wiped in one operation. Notice that the applicator is slightly tilted to put more pressure on the back part of the pad.

front of the applicator will apply the stain and the rear will wipe it. When using this method, dip only the front half of the pad into the stain. (Illus. 59)

You can also use a pad applicator to apply varnish to large flat surfaces such as doors or table tops. Use a good quality pad, preferably one that hasn't previously been used for any other material. When filling the pad with varnish, don't squeeze the pad as this will create air bubbles; just dip the pad into the tray. The pad won't hold as much varnish this way and so you will have to return it to the tray more often, but the resulting finish will be smoother.

Cleaning a pad applicator thoroughly is of prime importance. If any material is allowed to dry in the foam, the pad will be ruined. To clean the pad, pour a small amount of the appropriate thinner into the roller tray and repeatedly squeeze the pad against the bottom of the tray. Change the thinner and repeat until the thinner shows no trace of the stain or varnish. Next, fill the tray with soapy water and again squeeze the pad against the bottom of the tray. Finally, rinse the pad in clear water and squeeze dry. Set the pad on its back to dry. It may take a day or more for all of the water to evaporate from the pad after cleaning, so it cannot be reused for non-

water based products again until it is thoroughly dry. If you will be reusing it very soon, omit the water wash.

SPRAY EQUIPMENT

Applying a finish with spray equipment is probably the easiest way to achieve a uniform, even surface free of brush marks. It is possible to spray almost every finishing material available, from stains and sealers to varnish and lacquer. The only real disadvantage to spray equipment is the high initial investment required, but even that disadvantage is becoming smaller all the time as new low-cost machines are introduced.

Safety Precautions for Spraying

The place you set up your spray equipment is as important as the equipment itself. Spraying can produce hazardous fumes that can pose health problems, if adequate ventilation is not provided. In addition, the area you choose should be relatively clean and dust free to avoid contaminating the finished surface.

The ideal place to spray is in a professional

Illus. 60. A leg-type booth is suitable for spraying small objects. It doesn't take up a lot of space and it provides a working counter at a convenient height.

Illus. 61. A full-size spray booth gives you floor to ceiling space to spray large pieces of furniture.

spray booth. A spray booth incorporates an exhaust fan with a filter system to ensure adequate ventilation, and a dust-free atmosphere. Some booths use a water wash for the exhaust air to minimize air pollution as well. (Illus. 60, 61)

Lacking a spray booth, the next best alternative is to spray out of doors. Unless you have an elaborate exhaust system, it is hard to provide adequate ventilation indoors. When you spray outside, water down the area before setting up the spray equipment. This will keep down the dust. A slight breeze is good to provide air circulation. Another advantage to spraying outside is there is less chance that overspray will damage anything. When you spray, the air is filled with tiny droplets of the finishing material; this overspray can travel relatively long distances, and if it settles on a piece of furniture, for example, it will create a spot that is hard to remove.

If you are spraying a finish that contains flammable solvents, turn off any pilot lights in the area and don't smoke; the air will be filled with flammable fumes that can explode.

When you spray, wear a dust mask or a respirator. A dust mask will filter out the droplets of overspray that would otherwise be deposited in your lungs. However, a dust mask will not filter out fumes. If adequate ventilation has been provided, a dust mask will suffice; but if the air is also filled with fumes, a respirator that provides a flow of clean air should be used. (Illus. 62, 63, 64, 65)

Illus. 62. A dust mask filters out particles of overspray, but it doesn't protect against harmful fumes.

Illus. 63. The organic vapor mask uses a chemical filter to remove most common fumes from breathing air.

Illus. 64. An air-supplied mask provides the wearer with a constant supply of clean, fresh air. This type is necessary when ventilation is not adequate.

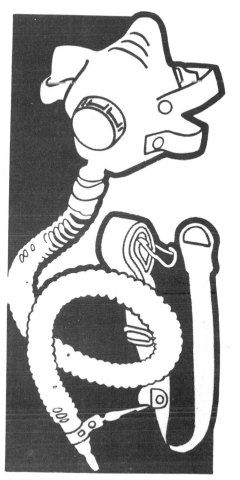

Illus. 65. The hood respirator provides the best protection against toxic fumes because it protects the eyes, nose, mouth and entire head.

Types of Spray Equipment

There are two main categories of spray equipment: air and airless. Air spray equipment atomizes the liquid to be sprayed with compressed air, while airless equipment uses a hydraulic pump to pressurize the liquid. Both types are available in a large range of sizes and prices from large industrial equipment to small home models.

Air spray equipment. There is a large variety of air spray equipment available, but all have one thing in common; they must be supplied compressed air by a separate compressor. Air compressors can be powered by

either electric or gasoline motors ranging from smaller than ¼ hp to over 15 hp. The air is compressed by either a reciprocating piston, much the same as an automobile

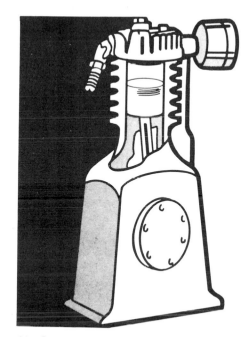

Illus. 66. Cutaway of a piston-type air compressor.

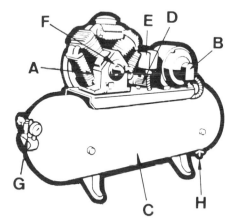

Illus. 67. Parts of a compressor: (A) compressor pump, (B) electric motor (or gasoline engine), (C) air storage tank (also called air receiver), (D) check valve (prevents back flow of air from tank), (E) pressure switch (turns motor off at preset pressure), (F) centrifugal pressure release (allows motor to start under less load—usually only on large compressors, (G) safety valve (bleeds off excess pressure), (H) drain valve (used to drain out water that condenses in the tank).

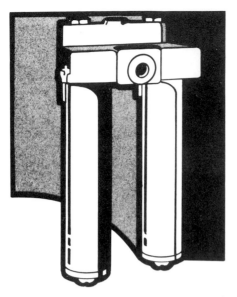

Illus. 68. An air condenser filters the air before it reaches the spray gun.

piston (Illus. 66), or by a rubber diaphragm. The air supplied directly from the compressor will be pulsating in pressure because of the action of the diaphragm or piston. To smooth out the pulsations and provide some air storage, an air tank is usually attached to larger compressors. When a tank is provided, there is usually a pressure switch on the compressor that turns off the motor when the tank is full. A relief valve should be incorporated in every compressor system to bleed off excess pressure. (Illus. 67)

When air is compressed, moisture from the atmosphere is also drawn into the system. This moisture will condense into water and can cause defects in a finish, if the water droplets are sprayed with the finish. To remove this water along with any oil that may have escaped from the compressor, an air condenser is used. The air condenser uses filters and separators to remove the contaminants from the air; the contaminants settle to the bottom of the condenser where a small drain allows them to be removed. (Illus. 68) If the spray equipment is used extensively, the air condenser should be drained once a day and thoroughly cleaned once a month. If the equipment is only used occasionally, the air condenser should be drained after each use.

Small compressors used for portable spray equipment usually provide barely enough pressure to operate the spray gun, so no means of reducing or regulating the pressure is provided. Larger compressors, however, provide much more pressure than needed to operate the spray gun, so a regulator must be used to reduce the pressure to a usable level. Different types of finishes require different pressure settings for best spraying results. (Illus. 69) Professional systems usually use an air transformer that combines the function of the regulator with the air condenser; a gauge is usually incorporated with the regulator so the pressure can be accurately set to any level. The air transformer usually has several air outlets that can be individually shut off; some also provide an outlet for unregulated air at line pressure. (Illus. 70)

Spray guns used with compressed air are of two main types: syphon and pressure

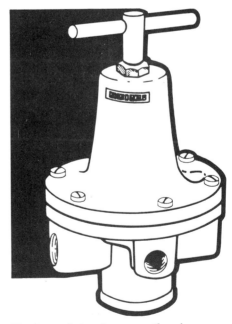

Illus. 69. A regulator decreases the air pressure to the proper setting for the material being applied.

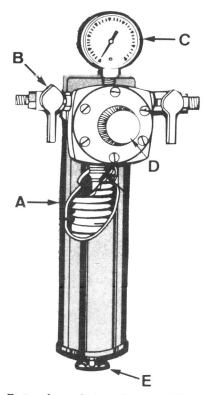

Illus. 70. Parts of an air transformer: (A) condenser, (B) outlet valve, (C) pressure gauge, (D) regulator, (E) drain valve.

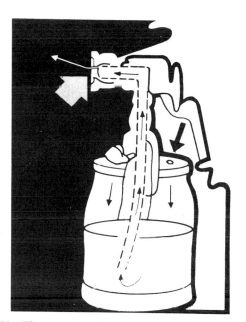

Illus. 72. The pressure-feed gun uses compressed air to force the liquid through the feed tube.

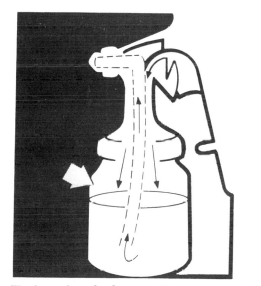

Illus. 71. A syphon-feed gun relies on atmospheric pressure entering through a vent hole to force the liquid up the feed tube.

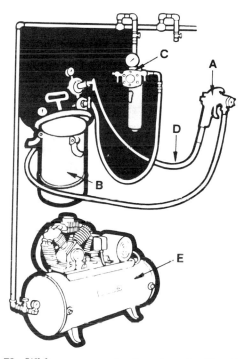

Illus. 73. With a pressure-feed system the liquid container (B) can be separate from the gun (A). Air is supplied from the compressor (E) through air transformer (C) to pressurize the liquid in the tank (B). The liquid flows through a feed hose to the gun (A). A separate air hose (D) delivers air to the gun to atomize the spray.

feed. A syphon-feed gun can be recognized by the fact that there is a small vent hole in the top of the liquid cup. The syphon gun operates on the same principle as an automobile carburetor. When rapidly moving air passes a restriction called a venturi, a small amount of suction is created. This suction is great enough to draw thin liquids up the feed tubes from the liquid cup. (Illus. 71) The main disadvantage of a syphon-feed gun is that thick liquids, such as varnish, must be thinned considerably before they can be sprayed. For this reason, a syphon-feed gun is best suited for applying thin materials like stain or lacquer.

The pressure-feed gun has a sealed liquid cup with no vent hole. Air pressure inside the liquid cup forces the finishing material up the feed tube. (Illus. 72) This enables the gun to handle much thicker liquids, making the pressure-feed gun more suitable for applying thicker materials such as varnish. Pressure-feed guns are available with attached liquid cups like a syphon-feed gun or with a detached liquid container. (Illus. 73) The detached container allows the operator more freedom of movement and can be larger, so it doesn't need to be filled as often.

Spray systems that use small compressors without pressure regulation frequently use a type of gun called a bleeder; this type allows air to escape from the gun at all times, maintaining a more or less even air pressure in the system. In a bleeder gun, the trigger controls only the flow of liquid, not the flow of air.

Once the liquid has been fed from the liquid cup to the head of the spray gun, it must be atomized into small droplets. This is accomplished by mixing the liquid with the pressurized air. There are two ways to do this: the external mix cap and the internal mix cap. With the external mix cap the liquid is forced out of a small orifice in the center of the cap as a small stream; jets of air from the sides of the cap are aimed at the stream of liquid. When the air jets hit the liquid, the stream is broken up into tiny droplets and fanned out into the proper pattern for efficient spraying. (Illus. 74) The external mix cap is especially well suited for spraying fast-drying materials like lacquer, because there is less chance of accumulating a buildup of material around the nozzle. The external mix cap also gives you accurate control of the spray pattern because you can vary the force of the air jets that fan out the liquid stream.

The internal mix cap mixes the air with the liquid inside the cap; the spray pattern is determined by the size and shape of the orifice that the air-liquid mixture is forced through. (Illus. 75)

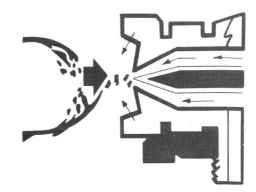

Illus. 74. The external mix cap uses two streams of air to fan out and atomize the liquid stream.

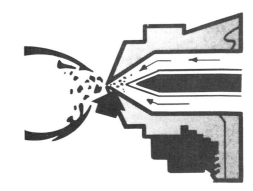

Illus. 75. An internal mix cap atomizes the liquid by forcing it through a very small orifice. The shape of the spray pattern is determined by the shape of the orifice.

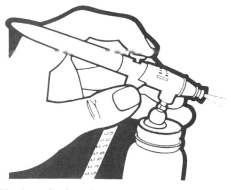

Illus. 76. An air brush gives precise control over placement and density of the spray.

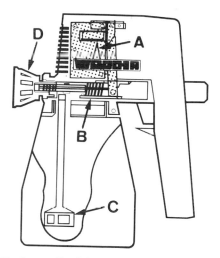

Illus. 77. A small airless sprayer: A small electric motor (A) contained in the gun operates a pump (B) that draws liquid up the feed tube (C) and forces it through an internal mix cap (D).

An air brush is a small spray gun that gives you precise control over the amount and location of the material sprayed. (Illus. 76) Air brushes are widely used for applying decorative details or for spraying small objects. Because the density of spray can be varied by a finger-tip control, an air brush can be very useful when applying stain to wood that varies widely in color. The stain can be applied heavier to the light areas.

Airless spray equipment. Airless spray equipment uses a hydraulic pump to pressurize the liquid to be sprayed. This pump may be a large external unit in the case of industrial airless sprayers, or in the case of small home units it can be contained inside the spray gun itself. The liquid is atomized by forcing it through a small orifice at high pressure. No air is mixed with the liquid.

The small home variety of airless sprayer is comparable to a syphon-feed gun in capabilities. (Illus. 77) The liquid to be sprayed must be thinned to allow the sprayer to handle it. Most units of this type require that the liquid be thinned to a very close tolerance for them to operate correctly. To achieve this, they come with a viscosity cup to gauge the viscosity of the liquid. A viscosity cup is a small cup that contains a measured amount of liquid. There is a small hole in the bottom of the cup. By timing how long it takes for all of the liquid to run out through the hole, the liquid's viscosity or thickness can be gauged. The manufacturer will recommend a specific time for the cup to empty. If it empties too slowly, the liquid must be thinned; if it empties too rapidly, the liquid has been thinned too much and additional unthinned liquid must be added.

Larger airless equipment has a distinct advantage over air equipment. The large pump can handle most finishing products unthinned or with very little thinning. This type of airless equipment is best suited for spraying large objects and long production runs. The finishing material can be drawn directly from its original container. The liquid is fed to the spray gun through a hose, so there is less operator fatigue because he only has to carry the weight of the spray gun. There is also less time lost refilling the liquid container. (Illus. 78) This type of airless equipment is not well suited for the jobs that only require a small amount of material to be sprayed before changing to another type of material, because it is fairly difficult to clean and requires a large amount of liquid to charge the lines. It is best used in situations where one type of liquid will be used to cover

Illus. 78. A large airless sprayer is similar to a pressure-feed gun. The liquid container is separate from the gun and usually can hold five gallons at a time. Some models make provision for drawing the liquid directly from the container it comes in. The pump can be driven by an electric motor, a gasoline engine, or an air motor.

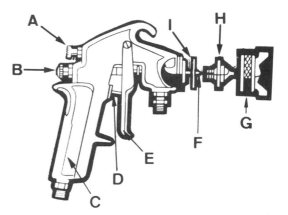

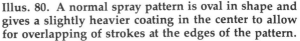

Illus. 79. Spray gun parts: (A) pattern control, (B) fluid control, (C) gun body, (D) air valve, (E) trigger, (F) fluid needle, (G) air cap, (H) fluid tip, (I) baffle.

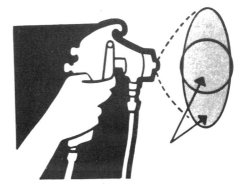

Illus. 80. A normal spray pattern is oval in shape and gives a slightly heavier coating in the center to allow for overlapping of strokes at the edges of the pattern.

a large surface or repeatedly used for many small objects. If the system will be used on a daily basis, most industrial airless sprayers can be left charged overnight so there is not a lot of time lost in cleanup.

Spraying Technique

No matter what type of equipment you use, the basic technique of spraying is the same. The first step is to adjust the gun so it is delivering the proper amount of liquid in the correct spray pattern. Point the gun at a large scrap board and test the spray pattern. Set the air pressure at the setting recommended for the material you are using. Most wood finishing materials should be applied at pressures under 50 pounds per square inch (PSI). Adjust the fluid control (Illus. 79) until you can get an even wet coat with the minimum amount of liquid. Opening the fluid control too much will result in runs and sags, especially for the beginning operator. Next adjust the spreader or pattern control to provide a long oval pattern. (Illus. 80) The fluid control may need some readjustment after the pattern has been set. Finally, set the pattern for the direction of travel. The length of the oval pattern should be at a 90 degree angle to the direction of travel. With an external mix cap this is easy to remember, because

you set the ears on the cap parallel to the direction of travel. If you will be making vertical strokes, the ears are set vertically; they are set horizontally if you will be moving the gun in horizontal strokes.

To apply the finish, hold the gun at a right angle to the surface at a distance of six to ten inches. (Illus. 81) It is important that the gun be held at a constant distance from the surface, because the finish achieved varies with distance. If the gun is too close, sags, runs, and ripples will result; but if it is too far away, the finish will be rough and uneven. A combination of wrist and shoulder movements is required to achieve a proper stroke with the gun. If the arm is simply pivoted at the shoulder or the hand pivoted at the wrist, the resulting motion will be an arc that will cause

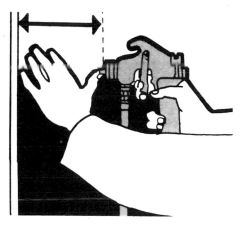

Illus. 81. You can estimate the correct distance to hold the gun from the surface for most work by spreading your hand in this manner.

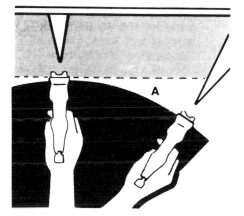

Illus. 82. The gun must remain parallel to the surface through the entire stroke. If the gun is arched as shown at (A) the film thickness of the finish will be thick in the middle and thinner at the edges.

the gun to be farther away from the surface at the beginning and end of each stroke. (Illus. 82) Instead, the gun must be maintained at a uniform distance from the surface throughout the stroke. Pull the trigger at the beginning of each stroke and release it at the end of the stroke before changing directions. After releasing the trigger at the end of the stroke, follow through on the stroke by continuing the motion of the gun slightly past the edge of the work. This follow-through will help you maintain a constant speed across the surface so there won't be a buildup

at the edge where you slowed down to change directions.

At the beginning of the next stroke, position the gun so that the pattern will overlap about one third of the previous stroke. Because the fan-out of the pattern deposits more material in the center than at the edges, the overlap will ensure an even coating.

Effective spraying requires advance planning. Whenever possible, position the work so that its largest area will be flat. This reduces the possibility of runs or sags. Objects to be sprayed should be supported by small blocks or nails driven partly into the bottom of the object to keep it up off the floor or spray table. This allows any finish that may accumulate at the bottom edge to drip off. Otherwise this excess finish would ooze under the object and glue it to the surface below. When all surfaces of an object must be sprayed, it is sometimes possible to hang the object from a wire.

Projects such as bookcases or shelf units that have many small openings are easier to spray if the finish is applied before they are assembled. That way all of the parts can be laid out flat, and the chance of overspray marring the completed finish of an adjacent surface is eliminated.

When spraying a horizontal surface with an airless gun that is supplied by a hose, the gun should be held at a right angle to the work. This is not possible with air or airless guns that carry the finish in a cup attached to the gun, because the liquid will spill out and the feed tube won't draw the liquid properly. So with this type of gun, hold it at approximately a 45 degree angle to the surface. Start the first stroke along the edge closest to you and aim the gun so that the overspray will land on the unfinished surface.

Spray corners first with the gun pointing directly at the point of the corner.

Vertical surfaces should be sprayed from the top down. Angle the gun so that you don't overspray on previously sprayed surfaces.

When you first begin to use a spray gun, you will more than likely have a few problems. Here is a list of the most common ones along with their probable causes (Illus. 83):

Runs and sags: A run is a large drip of finish that runs down a vertical surface; a sag is similar to a run only it covers a wider area. Both are caused by too much finish being deposited in one spot. Several errors in technique can cause runs and sags. The gun may have been moved too slowly or at an uneven speed. The feed may be set too heavy. The material may have been thinned too much, or the gun may have been held at an improper angle.

Sandpaper finish or orange peel: A sandpaper finish is rough like sandpaper rather than being smooth and glossy. An orange peel finish may have some gloss, but it is textured like an orange. Both can be caused by holding the gun too far away from the surface, using too little thinner or the wrong thinner, using too little air pressure with varnish or too much air pressure with lacquer. Allowing overspray to land on the surface of the work will also create a rough finish, especially with lacquer.

Ripples: A wavy or rippled surface is caused by holding the gun too close to the work or by setting the air pressure a bit too high.

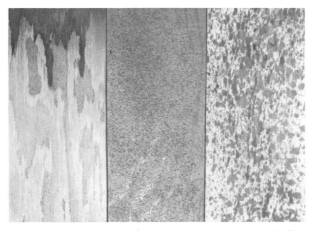

Illus. 83. Spraying problems: (A) runs, (B) rough finish, (C) sputtering.

Sputtering: If the gun sputters or spits blobs of finish, the liquid may not have been thinned enough. The vent in a syphon feed gun may be clogged. The mixing cap may be loose, or its seal damaged, or one of the packing nuts on the control needles may be loose or damaged.

Cleaning Spray Equipment

Cleaning spray equipment is not hard; but if it is not done thoroughly, the equipment will become clogged and require disassembly and very vigorous cleaning.

After each use, empty the cup of all remaining finish and fill the cup with thinner. Install the cup on the gun and shake it around to clean the cup lid and the top of the feed tube. Now simply spray the contents of the cup through the gun to clean the internal parts. If a lot of overspray has accumulated on the outside of the gun, wet a rag with thinner and wipe off the gun. Use a rag to clean the threads on the cup and the gun and wipe off the cup rubber gasket. On syphon-feed guns, make sure that the vent hole is clear. Remove the mixing cap and soak it in thinner for a few minutes, then wipe it dry. If a rubber O ring is used to seal the mixing cap, remove it and wipe it off; also clean the seat for the O ring and the threads to which the mixing cap attaches. If you follow this cleaning procedure, you should not need to disassemble the gun further.

If, however, the gun is put away without a thorough cleaning, you will probably have to completely disassemble it to get it working again. Remove all gaskets and packing rings and wipe them off with a rag dipped in solvent. Place only the metal parts in a shallow pan and cover them with lacquer thinner. Let the parts soak for about half an hour. Next put on some rubber or neoprene gloves and use a small brush to clean all of the parts. A pipe cleaner can be used to clean out the passageways in the gun body. Small orifices can be cleaned out with a wooden toothpick. Don't use wire or other metal objects to clean orifices because they may enlarge them or create burrs. As you reassemble the gun, apply a very small amount of lubricant to the parts shown in Illus. 84. Never use any lubricant that contains silicones because this can lead to a condition known as "fish eyes," small round depressions to appear in the top coat caused by a tiny amount of silicone contaminating the finish.

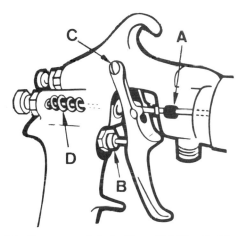

Illus. 84. Spray-gun lubrication. (A) The fluid needle packing should be given a few drops of light oil occasionally to keep it soft. (B) The air valve packing also requires light oil. (C) Light machine oil will keep the trigger operating smoothly. (D) The fluid needle spring gets a light coat of petroleum jelly.

Aerosol Cans

A wide range of finishing products are available in aerosol cans. This can be a good alternative for the person who doesn't have spray equipment and yet would like to achieve the type of finish offered by spraying. Care should be taken when choosing an aerosol product; inferior types will produce very poor results while a quality product will give results that are comparable to those achieved with a spray gun. The spray head or valve is of prime importance in producing good results. The best type has an adjustable

fan pattern. Rotating a small plastic square on the tip of the valve changes the fan pattern from horizontal to vertical. (Illus. 85) Most spray heads lack this feature though and only provide a round spray pattern. Good results can be achieved even with the standard type head if a good quality valve is used. About the only way to be sure if a particular product uses a good valve is to buy one can and experiment with it. A good valve will be easy to press; it will produce a fine evenly distributed spray, and it won't sputter or spit out blobs of finish.

If you can't find the finishing product you need in an aerosol can, you can get a special type of aerosol that has a small glass jar that can be filled with any liquid. Thin the liquid the same as you would for use in a syphon-feed spray gun. (Illus. 86)

The technique of spraying with an aerosol can is basically the same as spraying with a spray gun. Maintain a uniform distance from the work throughout the stroke. Lift your finger from the valve at the end of the stroke and follow through. All of the procedures previously discussed for spraying, using a spray gun, apply to aerosol cans as well. The feed tube in an aerosol can is bent just like

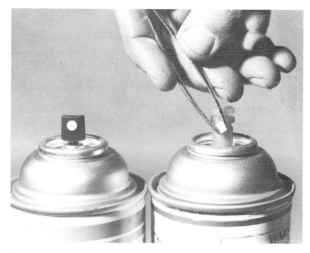

Illus. 85. An ordinary aerosol spray head (left) produces a round pattern while an adjustable fan spray head (right) gives results comparable to a spray gun. A pair of tweezers makes adjusting the valve easier.

Illus. 86. This type of aerosol allows you to spray any material that you would use with a spray gun.

must face to take advantage of the bend in the tube. (Illus. 87)

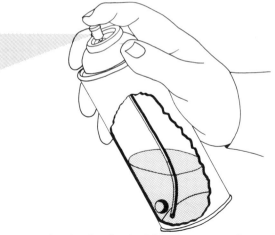

Illus. 87. The feed tube inside of an aerosol can is bent to allow it to pick up the liquid even when the can is almost empty and tilted 45 degrees. Notice the agitator ball. It helps mix pigmented material. Clear finishes may not have an agitator ball.

the feed tube in a spray gun; this allows you to tilt the can to about 45 degrees to spray horizontal surfaces. There will usually be an inked mark on the rim of the can near the valve; this indicates the direction the valve

3 · Staining and Filling

Each species of wood has a natural color that is enhanced by the application of a clear finish. Individual boards will have slight color variations. Also, the effects of time can change the color of a board. As the wood that has been left unfinished or given a clear finish ages, a natural darkening occurs; this acquired color is called patina. As time went on, people became accustomed to the patina achieved over hundreds of years and wanted to duplicate it on new work without waiting for it to occur naturally, so the process of staining was born. Today stains are used to color almost all wood that receives a clear finish. However, there are some woods such as walnut, cherry, rosewood, mahogany, and oak that are so beautifully colored naturally that they are often left in their natural state and given only a clear finish. In fact, most other varieties of wood are stained to imitate the natural color of these naturally beautiful woods. Even these woods are often stained, not so much to change the color, but to enhance the grain and even the color from board to board.

Of course taste in furniture and woodwork is partly a matter of what is in fashion; at times light-colored wood is in fashion and the light woods like birch and maple are left unstained and dark woods are bleached or given a limed finish. At other times, dark woods are in fashion and everything is stained dark.

Filling is another process that can change the natural characteristics of a piece of wood. Some woods are closed grained, which means they have pores so small that they are virtually undetectable. Pine, cherry, birch, and maple are closed-grain woods. (Illus. 88) These woods will take a finish that is extremely smooth and glossy. On the other hand, open-grained woods such as walnut, oak, and mahogany have large pores that are a prominent feature of the grain. (Illus. 89) These woods lend themselves well to satin finishes that allow the texture of the wood to show through. But if a smooth gloss finish is desired, the pores must be filled level with the surface.

Types of Stains

Wood can be stained with either pigments or dyes. Pigments are opaque substances such as minerals that are ground to a fine powder. The pigments are suspended in a liquid to be applied to the wood. To impart color, they form a thin layer on the surface of the wood. Because they are opaque and lie on the surface of the wood, they tend to hide some of the details of the grain.

The dyes used to stain woods are derivatives of coal tar called aniline dyes. They are

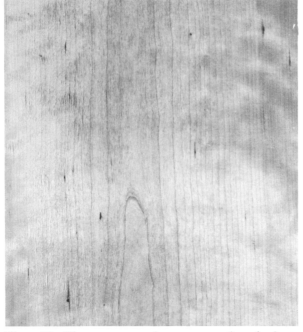

Illus. 88. Cherry veneer is an example of close-grained (fine-textured) wood. Note gum deposits.

Illus. 89. Black walnut veneer is an example of open-grained (coarse-grained) wood. Note flat sliced knots.

transparent and color the wood by soaking into the individual fibres. Because of this characteristic, they let all of the grain detail show through.

Both types have desirable characteristics, so the choice must be based on what effect you want to achieve on a particular project. Pigmented stains tend to enhance the pattern of the pores because more pigments will accumulate in them, while dye stains will accentuate variations in color and play down the pore pattern. You will have to analyze the individual boards you are working with to determine which type would produce the most pleasing effect.

The liquid (technically called the "vehicle") used in making the stain also affects how the stain will perform. Water, alcohol, and oil are commonly used. Pigments and dyes are also mixed with lacquer or varnish to make special-purpose stains.

The most commonly used types of stains are (Illus. 90): Pigmented oil stain, pigmented latex stain, penetrating oil stain, water stain, spirit stain, non-grain-raising stain, shading stain, and varnish stain.

Pigmented oil stain

Probably the most common type of stain sold for home use is pigmented oil stain; it is sometimes called wiping stain, because wiping is an important part of its application. Pigmented oil stain contains finely ground pigments suspended in a mixture of linseed oil, solvents, driers and other components commonly found in varnish.

The major virtue of this type of stain is that it is extremely forgiving. It is slow drying, giving you plenty of time to work; and since it is more of a surface coating than a penetrating one, lap marks and uneven areas can be smoothed out by wiping. Pigmented oil stains are very color stable, so there is no need to worry that they will fade in strong light as some other stains will. They are also available in a wide selection of colors ready mixed, so there is little preparation involved.

Pigmented oil stain can be applied with a

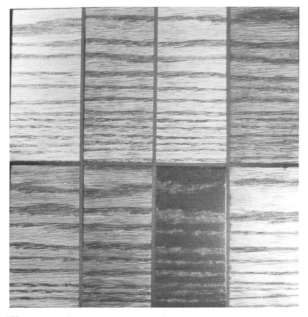

Illus. 90. Common types of stain. Left to right, top row: pigmented oil, latex, penetrating oil, water stain. Bottom row: spirit stain, NGR stain, shading stain, varnish stain.

brush, by spraying, or with a cloth. No matter how it is applied, you should wipe it with a cloth after application to produce the best effect. The wiping process is the most important step in applying a wiping stain. If it is not done correctly, the wood will have a muddy look and most of the grain will be obscured. Use a clean, lint-free cloth folded into a pad. Wipe in long even strokes in the direction of the grain. Occasionally refold the pad so that a clean surface is exposed. Your goal in wiping should be a uniform appearance that gives you the color desired without hiding the natural beauty of the wood. (Illus. 91) The color intensity can be varied by how hard you wipe the stain or how long you let the stain sit on the wood before you wipe it. Leaving the stain on the wood for only a short time and wiping it off very hard will produce a light color, while wiping lightly after the stain has been on the wood for several minutes will produce a darker color.

Pigmented oil stains are very useful when there are variations in the color of the lumber used in the project. You can even out the colors by wiping harder in the dark areas and using less pressure in the light areas. In some cases, you can wipe the entire surface evenly at first, let the stain dry for about half an hour, then wipe over the dark areas again to bring them closer in shade to the rest of the wood. Sometimes it may be necessary to wet the rag with a little paint thinner or turpentine to remove as much of the pigmentation as is necessary.

The pigments in this type of stain will settle to the bottom of the container after a period of time, so you must thoroughly stir the contents before use and occasionally during use if you are working on a large project.

The pigments will accumulate more heavily in depressions in the wood, so any scratches or dents will show up as dark areas in the finish.

Oil stains are usually formulated to be compatible with most top coats, but they are most compatible with varnish. Usually you should let the stain dry for 24 hours before applying any further finish. However, if there is some reason that you must hurry, you can usually apply a varnish coat after several hours. Check the container label to make sure.

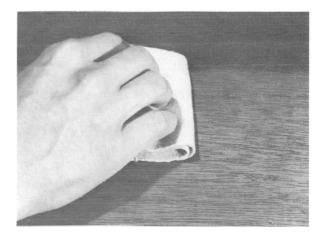

Illus. 91. Wiping is an important procedure for pigmented oil stains.

Pigmented latex stain

Although it is not as widely available as pigmented oil stain, latex stain is becoming increasingly popular because it is nonflammable, it produces no harmful fumes, and water can be used for cleanup.

Latex stain performs almost exactly like pigmented oil stain, except that it dries faster. Even though they are water soluble, most latex stains are formulated so they won't raise the grain of the wood as water stains do. To preserve this property, apply the stain straight from the can without any thinning. If the directions on the can don't tell you whether the stain will raise the grain or not, test the stain on a piece of scrap wood to make sure. If it does raise the grain, the wood should be treated as described in the section on water stain. Latex stain is applied just like pigmented oil stain, but it dries more rapidly so it should be wiped sooner. If the color is too dark, you can lighten it by wiping with a cloth dampened with water. However, this method will tend to raise the grain.

Penetrating oil stain

When dyes rather than pigments are mixed in oil, the resulting stain is called a penetrating oil stain. The stain penetrates into the fibres of the wood rather than coating the surface. Because the dyes are transparent, the stain does not obscure the grain as much as a pigmented stain will.

Penetrating oil stains can be applied with a brush (Illus. 92) or rag and wiped just like a pigmented oil stain. Penetrating oil stain can also be applied with spray equipment. When it is sprayed on, no wiping is necessary if the color is uniform.

Some of the dyes used in oil stains have a tendency to fade in direct sunlight, so they should not be used for applications that will receive long exposures to the sun, such as exterior doors. Using a top coat that has an

Illus. 92. Penetrating oil stains can be applied with a brush, or they can be wiped on with a rag.

ultraviolet shield will help to prevent fading.

One of the most popular types of penetrating oil stain combines the stain with a tung oil or Danish oil finish. This system allows for staining and finishing in one operation. Caution: they are flammable and the vapors can be harmful.

Water stain

Water stain is considered the ultimate when clarity of grain and permanence are desired. A water stain comes as a dry powder that must be mixed by the user with water. The dyes used in water stains are the most transparent and most fade-resistant of the anilines.

Water stains soak deep into the wood, deeper than any other type of stain. Additional coats of stain can be used to deepen the color without fear of obscuring the grain.

Although they have many advantages, water stains are not appropriate for all applications. Because water is used in the formula, the stain will raise the grain when it is applied unless the wood is specially prepared beforehand. As wood is planed and sanded, the fibres are flattened down into the surface. Water causes these fibres to stand up again, creating a rough fuzzy texture called raised grain. (Illus. 93) This prob-

Illus. 93. Applying water to wood creates a rough fuzzy texture called raised grain (left). A light sanding will remove these raised fibres (right).

Illus. 94. Water stain must be mixed with warm water before use. A small packet of the dried stain usually makes one quart of liquid.

lem is easy to correct. Simply wipe a damp sponge over the surface of the wood to raise the grain before applying the stain, then use fine sandpaper to smooth off the raised fibres. When the stain is applied, the surface will remain smooth since all of the fibres that would have stood up have been sanded off.

If more than one coat of stain will be used, the pre-sponging can be deleted; instead sand the first coat of stain. Water stains should not be used over thin veneers, because they will cause them to swell and buckle.

Water stains are usually sold in small packets that will make a quart of stain. To prepare the stain, heat a quart of water to boiling and let it cool slightly. Add the contents of the packet (or one ounce if you buy the powder in bulk) to the water and stir. (Illus. 94) Let the mixture cool and strain it through a piece of tight-weave cloth. Store the mixed stain in a glass or plastic container. Don't store it in metal. The stain tends to oxidize metal, and the resulting compounds in the stain will create unintended colors to appear when the stain is applied to the wood.

Applying water stain takes more skill than oil stains because of a tendency to show lap marks. The best way to apply a water stain is with a spray gun. You can also use a brush, rag, or sponge to apply the stain, but it will take practice before you will be able to apply the stain evenly. No wiping is necessary with water stains, so the stain must be applied perfectly the first time.

Spirit stain

Spirit stains are similar to water stains in appearance, but there is one important difference. The dyes used in spirit stains fade rapidly in strong light. Spirit stains have the advantages of not raising the grain as water stains do. They also dry rapidly, allowing you to apply other finishing coats the same day. Because of the rapid drying time, they don't soak into the wood as deep as water stains and they are more difficult to apply. The fading problem can be partially overcome by using a top coat that contains an ultraviolet shield, but generally spirit stains are not used for complete pieces of furniture. Spirit stains are most useful as touchup stains; the stain will penetrate through some top coats, particularly shellac, so it can be used to touch up an area that has already been sealed. Spirit stain comes as a dry powder; to prepare it for use, mix the powder with alcohol. The type of alcohol sold as shellac thinner works well. After the stain is mixed, store it in a dark brown glass container and keep it out of direct light.

Non-grain-raising stain

If you combine the advantages of a water stain with the advantages of a spirit stain you come up with a non-grain-raising stain, commonly referred to, as NGR stain. The secret of the NGR stain is in its solvent, so they are only sold as liquids. The dyes used are similar to the dyes used in water stains, so they are transparent and light fast. The trick is to use a mixture of solvents like glycol, acetone, toluol and alcohol (all flammable) to dissolve the dyes rather than water. The result is a stain with the clarity and permanence of a water stain that won't raise the grain.

NGR stains dry almost as fast as spirit stains, so they are rather difficult to apply evenly with a brush. The preferred method of applying NGR stains is with a spray gun. For this reason, they are not commonly sold as a do-it-yourself product, but they are widely used in the furniture industry. You can buy small quantities of NGR stain from several mail order woodworking firms that cater to advanced home craftsmen. If you must apply a NGR stain with a brush, add some retarder that is sold specifically for that purpose to slow down the drying time.

Shading stains

Shading stains are actually a surface coating made of lacquer mixed with dyes or pigments. They are widely used in the furniture industry because they can produce uniform results on a variety of woods. Much of the inexpensive-to-medium-price-range furniture sold today has been stained with a shading stain. This enables the manufacturer to use several of the less expensive hard woods in the same piece of furniture and finish it to a uniform color. Shading stains can only be applied by spraying.

You can apply shading stains to bare wood or wood that has already had another type of stain applied.

Shading stains are very useful if you are trying to match a piece of factory built furniture. Aerosol cans of the product are available for those who lack spray equipment.

There are two major drawbacks to the shading stains. First, they will hide the grain of the wood, especially if applied in a heavy coat. This can sometimes be an advantage if you are trying to match two pieces of wood with very different grain patterns. The second drawback is that the stain will wear off of areas that receive a lot of rubbing like chair arms or table corners. Because this is a surface coating, the worn areas will be much lighter than the surrounding wood.

Shading stains are frequently used to achieve an effect called glazing. This is most

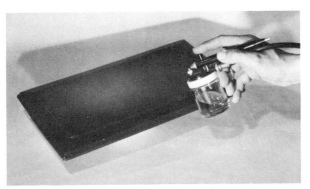

Illus. 95. Shading stains are frequently used in a process called glazing. The stain is sprayed around the edges of a panel to darken them and give the panel an antique look.

often used on cabinet doors or drawer fronts. The entire surface is stained to a uniform color, then a shading stain of a slightly darker color is sprayed around the edges. The spray gun is pointed at an angle towards the center of the work so that the edges receive the heaviest coat of spray and the coating tapers off so that it gradually blends with the base color at the center of the panel. (Illus. 95) Glazing was originally developed to try to duplicate the look of antique furniture that has the finish worn off in the center of a door, but it has now become a technique that is used on modern as well as antique reproduction furniture.

Varnish stains

A varnish stain is similar to a shading stain, only the color is added to a varnish instead of lacquer. Varnish stains are sometimes promoted as a one-step finish, but they really don't produce as nice a finish as can be achieved by using a separate stain and varnish. The trouble with trying to get the final finish in one step is that you can't control the stain by wiping and still maintain a good surface in the varnish. Varnish stains are useful for touch-up work and when a special effect is needed; for example, much of the furniture made during the 1930's through the 1950's used a finish that looks a lot like varnish stain. If you are trying to duplicate the finish on such an item, varnish stain will work well. The best way to apply a varnish stain is with a spray gun or from an aerosol can. Even though you can theoretically let a varnish stain stand as a complete finish, better results are achieved if you apply a clear top coat of varnish over the stain.

STAINING TECHNIQUE

The stain you choose to use and the way you apply it play a major role in how the completed finish will look. Illustrations 96 and 97 show examples of two different stain-

Illus. 96. The variation in color between boards in this chest emphasizes the fancy cabinet work.

ing techniques. The chest shown in Illus. 96 would lose much of its charm if the color variations between the different boards were covered up; while the bedroom set in Illus. 97 relies on a uniformity of color to give the set a traditional and unified appearance. In both cases, the final finish would not have been as well done if a different stain or method of application had been used.

One of the most important techniques in staining is experimentation. Always try a stain on a scrap of wood of the same type as the piece you are finishing to see if the effect produced is what you wanted. Also experiment with different methods of application on scrap wood. The effect that a stain will have on a given piece of wood is hard to predict without experimenting first. The color samples that the stain manufacturers provide are only a guide, because each species of wood takes a stain differently, and even individual boards of the same species will vary in how they stain.

Illus. 97. The uniformity of color in this bedroom set gives the furniture a traditional, unified appearance.

When you begin to stain the actual project, start on an inconspicuous area first, so if you are unhappy with the result there is still time to change the stain.

Always apply and wipe stains with the grain. This makes any lap marks less conspicuous.

Oil stains and latex stains should be applied heavily at first to allow for wiping. Water stain, spirit stain and NGR stain should be applied more sparingly. If you are brushing, don't use a full wet brush; the brush should be somewhat dry. Apply the stain from the brush as far as it will go without excessive brushing. Don't try to wring out the last drop of stain before refilling the brush.

When using a wiping stain, work with one area of the project at a time; for example, apply the stain to one door of a cabinet and wipe it before applying the stain to the next door. If you applied the stain to the entire project at once, there would be a variation in color between the parts you wiped first and those that were wiped last. This is because it takes longer to wipe the stain properly than

it does to apply it, so the last part to be wiped has had the stain on it for a longer period of time. If you have to let the stain set on the wood a long time before wiping, you can apply the stain to another section while you are waiting for the first to set, if you time your work carefully so that all sections receive an equal amount of setting time.

A pad applicator will make the job of applying almost any type of stain easier. Pad applicators work very well with wiping stains; and the application and wiping can even be done in one step in some cases, as was described in Chapter 2. Pad applicators also simplify the task of obtaining an even lap-free coat of water stain if you can't apply it with a spray gun.

End grain will absorb more stain than other parts of the project and will show up darker. In many instances this is not objectionable. Some feel that this is a mark of quality because it indicates that the wood used is solid. (Plywood with veneered edges never shows end grain.) However, if the color difference is extreme, you may want to pretreat the end grain to make it less absorbent. For most stains you can apply a thin coat of shellac to the end grain to limit the amounts of stain it will absorb or apply a coat of Danish oil or boiled linseed oil to the end grain. This is especially well suited for use with oil stains. You can decrease the amount of water stain that end grain absorbs by pre-wetting it with clear water immediately before staining.

FILLING

Woods such as oak, walnut, ash, and mahogany have large pores in their surface. Because of this, they are called open-grained woods. If you want to produce a smooth-as-glass finish on an open-grained wood, you will have to fill the pores. (Illus. 98) Of course, it is not always desirable to have a filled surface; sometimes the style of the furniture requires that the texture of the wood shows through. For example, oak is commonly left unfilled when a textured matte finish is desired. Contemporary walnut furniture is also usually left unfilled. Whether you fill the pores or not is purely a matter of personal taste and the style of the furniture

being finished. Unfilled wood is usually given a satin finish, while filled wood looks good with either a high gloss or a satin finish.

The product used to fill the pores is called paste filler; it is a mixture of linseed oil, dryers, and silex. Silex is a mineral that has been ground to a fine powder. Paste filler is available in several colors as well as natural. Usually the filler is applied after the wood has been stained, but it is possible to apply natural filler first and then stain the wood: this will only work if an oil stain is used. When applying filler over a stained surface, choose a color that is slightly darker than the color of the stain. This is not a hard-and-fast rule. You can use a lighter filler, but a darker one usually looks better. If you can't find a colored filler that suits your needs, you can tint natural filler with Japan colors or universal tinting colors. You can achieve dramatic and unusual effects by using contrasting fillers to emphasize the pore patterns. (Illus. 99)

Paste filler as it comes from the can is in a concentrated form; before it can be used, it must be thinned with turpentine or paint thinner. Thin the filler to the consistency of very thick paint. You should be able to brush

Illus. 98. The oak sample on the left has many large pores visible. The sample on the right has been filled.

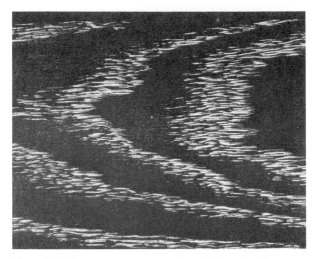

Illus. 99. You can use contrasting fillers for dramatic effects. In this case the oak sample was stained black, and white filler was used to fill the pores.

it easily, but don't thin it too much or it won't fill the pores correctly.

Applying filler may slightly change the color of the wood. Before applying the filler, test it on a scrap of wood that has been stained with the same stain as the wood you intend to fill. If the filler changes the color of the stain in a way that you don't like, seal the surface of the wood with a thin coat of shellac before applying the filler.

Apply the filler with a brush, working it into the pores by brushing cross grain. Stir the container of filler occasionally, because the solids will tend to settle to the bottom. Don't fill a large area all at once; work with small sections so all of the excess filler can be removed before it dries. Let the filler dry 5 to 20 minutes until it becomes dull.

When the surface of the filler looks dull, use a piece of cheesecloth to wipe the excess from the wood. Wipe across the grain to pack the filler into the pores, then use a clean cloth and wipe with the grain until there isn't any filler left on the surface; but try not to remove the filler from the pores.

Very intricate pieces are hard to fill, because it's so hard to get all of the excess filler out of all of the small nooks and crannies. In most cases, it's best not to fill intricately shaped or carved pieces; but if you must, be sure to remove every trace of filler from the surface. You can use a stiff brush to get a lot of it, but finally you will have to resort to a small dowel that has been sharpened to a point to remove the last traces from the small recesses.

There is another method of applying filler that will produce a very smooth surface. Apply the filler as previously described, let it dry for about five minutes, then wipe most of it off with a rag. Let the remaining filler dry until it is well set, usually several hours, then sand off the remaining filler with 600 grit wet-or-dry sandpaper. The sandpaper will clog up frequently, but you can clean it with a wire brush and reuse it. This method works best when the filler is applied to wood that has not been stained; if the wood has been stained, be very careful not to sand through the stain to bare wood. Let the filler dry at least 24 hours before proceeding with any other finishing steps. If a top coat is applied too soon, the filler won't dry properly; it may turn grey or it may lift the top coat.

4 · Protective Coatings

A wood surface that is not protected by a coating is susceptible to damage from water, natural aging, abrasion, and dirt. To protect the wood from these elements some type of protective coating is usually applied.

There are a wide range of protective coatings available. Each has uses for which it is best suited. Some are more durable than others, some enhance the beauty of the wood better than others, and some possess qualities that adapt them for special purposes. The protective coating is usually applied over a coat of stain, but sometimes a clear coating is all that is necessary to bring out the natural beauty of the wood.

Protective coatings can be classified as one of several general types: penetrating finishes, varnish, lacquer, shellac, two-part finishes, paint, or protective stains.

PENETRATING FINISHES

Penetrating finishes are one of the easiest for the novice to apply, and yet they produce such good results that they are the choice of many professionals. Penetrating finishes are marketed under several names: Danish oil, penetrating oil, or tung oil finish are commonly used terms.

Penetrating finishes soak into the wood and harden and seal the top surface of the wood to form the protective barrier. This ability to penetrate the wood surface gives these finishes three inherent advantages. A penetrating finish will not chip or flake off the surface, and scratches and dents are not as visible because the finish extends under the top surface of the wood. The finish also hardens the wood; making it less susceptible to damage. Some penetrating finishes are nontoxic when dry, making them safe to use on food-related items or children's furniture.

Surface preparation is of extreme importance when using a penetrating finish, because the surface of the wood will become the top surface of the finish. For this reason, you should use a finer grit sandpaper for the final sanding than is necessary with surface coatings. This property is a definite advantage for the inexperienced woodfinisher, because it makes it easy to achieve a highly professional-looking smooth surface without worrying about brush marks, laps, sags, runs, or dust. The surface of the completed finish will be just as smooth as the surface of the wood. (Illus. 100)

Penetrating finishes are particularly well suited for carvings because they won't build up in the carving details and they let the natural sheen left by sharp cutting tools show in the final finish. Penetrating oil finishes are available in aerosol cans that make it even

Illus. 100. Penetrating finishes are ideal when an ultra-smooth finish is desired.

Illus. 101. Aerosol cans make it easy to apply penetrating oil to intricate carvings.

easier to apply the finish to intricately carved surfaces. (Illus. 101)

Tung Oil

Tung oil is one of the major ingredients in most penetrating finishes. It is also called China nut oil, China wood oil, or nut oil. It is a natural oil obtained from the nut of the tung tree. It is capable of being polymerized into a natural plastic. It is frequently used as an ingredient in paint and varnish. It produces a finish that is waterproof and is not affected by alcohol, fruit acids, carbonated drinks, or acetone.

Tung oil is one of the more expensive ingredients in a finish, so it is used in varying concentrations in different products. Products containing high amounts of tung oil will produce a very good finish, and they possess the ability to build to a high gloss with successive coats; but the novice will find that products that contain less tung oil may be easier to use because they contain other ingredients that make the application easier.

Natural tung oil can be modified by a process called cooking. Cooked oil is faster drying and produces a harder, glossier surface because its molecules have been polymerized. By combining natural tung oil with cooked tung oil and other ingredients, sev-

eral types of tung oil finish can be produced.

Tung oil sealer is a deep penetrating product that contains about 20 percent cooked oil. It is used to seal and fill the pores of the wood deep below the surface. It is not used alone but provides a base for other tung oil products. All penetrating oils can be used as their own sealer; some recommend thinning the first coat; others don't. A separate sealer coat is only necessary when very deep penetration is needed.

Low luster finish is used to produce a finish that is practically flat, with very little gloss. It allows all of the wood's texture to show. These type of finishes contain about 25 percent cooked oil. They dry rapidly and are very easy to apply. They produce the type of finish that is associated with Danish modern furniture. They penetrate the surface deeply and will wear well in applications that receive a lot of traffic, such as floors and countertops, because as the surface is worn away the wood below still contains finish. Additional coats will increase the durability and patina of the finish, but they do not build to a high gloss.

Medium lustre finish contains approximately 35 percent cooked oil. It produces more gloss with fewer coats than the low lustre finishes and creates a harder surface; however, it doesn't penetrate as deeply. Additional coats will build to produce a glossy surface and hide some surface texture. It is about the same as low lustre finish in ease of application.

High gloss finish, sometimes called gun stock oil. This type contains over 50 percent cooked oil. It will build to a high gloss. It doesn't penetrate the wood as deeply as the others, and it requires more skill to apply. The material must be worked while it is still completely fluid; it begins to gel soon after application and can get very tacky. If the oil has not been completely applied before it begins to gel, it will show lap marks and unevenness in the finish.

Pure tung oil finish is the name usually used to designate an oil that contains almost exclusively natural tung oil with only a small amount of thinners added. It doesn't have any cooked oil in the formula. This type is preferred by many experienced finishers. It is more difficult to apply than finishes with additional ingredients, and it dries slower than those with cooked oils. But the quality of the finish produced is very high.

Other Penetrating Oils

Soybean oil, perilla oil, oiticica oil, linseed oil, safflower oil, sunflower oil, and synthetics like polyurethane are also used in the manufacture of penetrating oil finishes. Each manufacturer uses a different formula for its penetrating finish. If a finish is not advertised as high in tung oil, it likely contains some of these other oils, although at least a small amount of tung oil is used in virtually all penetrating finishes. Tung oil is considered the best overall oil for penetrating finishes, but the other oils each possess individual qualities that, when properly blended, can provide desirable characteristics to a penetrating finish. Don't rule out a product just because it isn't entirely made from tung oil; try different brands and formulas. You may prefer one that blends several oils.

Penetrating oils are often mixed with dyes and pigments to create a product that colors the wood and finishes it all in one step. Unlike some other so-called one-step finishes, this type really produces quality results. The oil is applied in exactly the same manner as natural colored oils; you can apply as many coats as you like without fear of obscuring the grain of the wood. When you have achieved the desired shade, you can stop or you can apply additional coats of clear oil.

Salad bowl oil is used to protect wood that will be used in food handling and preparation. Any wood that will be used in this manner should be finished with an oil that is FDA approved for use in contact with food. Some finishers use ordinary salad oil for this purpose, but this is not usually a satisfactory finish because the oil can turn rancid; so it is best to use an oil made specifically for the purpose.

Applying penetrating finishes

Penetrating finishes are usually applied with a rag, but they can be brushed or sprayed. Cover the wood with a generous amount of the oil and let it soak into the wood for about ten minutes. Reapply oil to any areas that have soaked in all of the oil applied. If you desire a very smooth finish and want to fill the grain of open-grained woods, flood the surface with oil and use 600 grit wet-or-dry sandpaper to wet-sand the surface. The sanding dust combined with the oil will produce a filler that will fill the pores. Steel wool is sometimes recommended for this purpose, but small particles of the wool will accumulate in the pores as well as the filler; so sandpaper is preferred. Before the oil begins to dry and become tacky, wipe all of the excess from the wood with a clean lint-free cloth. This method works well on woods like walnut or cherry that have relatively small pores. Woods like oak or mahogany that have larger pores may need an additional filler. You can use silex paste filler with a penetrating oil.

Apply one coat of the finish and let it dry, then thin some paste filler with the penetrating finish and apply it according to the directions given in Chapter 3. Pumice can also be used to fill the pores. Apply a coat of oil to the wood then sprinkle a little pumice onto it. Sand the wet surface with 600 grit wet-or-dry sandpaper. The sanding will make a paste of wood dust mixed with pumice that will blend with the color of the wood and fill the pores. Continue sanding until the pores are full, adding pumice if necessary. When you are finished sanding, wipe off any remaining filler with a rag.

You can apply as many additional coats of the oil as you desire to achieve the look you want. Let each coat dry between coats. Drying times differ from brand to brand, so check the label for exact instructions.

After the final coat is dry, burnish the surface by rubbing vigorously with a clean soft cloth or a piece of lamb's wool. You can leave the surface as is or apply a coat of wax.

Note: Penetrating oils dry by a process called oxidation. This means that the oils combine with oxygen from the air to harden. Rags used to apply the oil should be disposed of in sealed metal containers, because the oxidation process can create enough heat to cause the rags to burst into flames if they are left in a pile after use. This is called spontaneous combustion. *You should be careful of spontaneous combustion whenever disposing of rags that have been used with any finishing material that contains oil.*

Because these oils dry by combining with oxygen rather than by evaporation, you should keep the amount of oxygen in the container to a minimum. A full container of oil allows little room for oxygen, but a partially empty one may allow enough oxygen to remain inside to gel the contents. There are several ways to expel the oxygen from the container. If the container is flexible plastic, squeeze the sides together until the oil comes up to the top and then put on the lid. Metal

and glass containers require different techniques. Some people add glass marbles to the container to fill up the space. An easier method is to hold your breath for a while then blow into the container just before closing the lid. Your exhaled breath contains less oxygen than air, because your body consumes the oxygen. If you will be reusing the oil in only a few days, it is not necessary to worry about leaving oxygen in the container; but if you will be storing a penetrating oil finish for a long time in a partially empty container, removing the oxygen will ensure that the product will still be usable when you need it again.

Maintaining and Repairing Oil Finishes

One of the main advantages of an oil finish is that it is very easy to keep the finish looking brand new. An additional coat of finish can be applied at any time to bring the lustre back. After cleaning the surface, apply the finish like furniture polish. Wipe it on with a rag and buff it out. Damaged areas can be repaired by applying more oil to the area. If the wood is solid rather than veneered, dents, scratches and burn marks can be sanded out and additional finish applied. Small defects are removed best by applying oil to the area and wet-sanding the defect with 600 grit wet-or-dry paper. Larger de-

Illus. 102. A scratch in the surface of a penetrating oil finish can be repaired easily.

fects may require that a coarser paper be used first to remove the damaged wood, then use the 600 grit to achieve the final finish. (Illus. 102, 103, 104)

VARNISH

Varnish is made from natural and synthetic oils and resins. It is a surface coating that builds up a layer on top of the wood instead of penetrating deeply. Varnish is highly regarded for its durability and ease of application. It uses slow-evaporating solvents that enable it to be brushed on with more success than faster-drying products. Varnish can also be applied with spray equipment.

Varnishes are blended for many different applications; there is not one universal varnish. The one you should choose depends on the application you intend it for.

Natural oil varnishes are classified by the amount of oil they contain; those with a lot of oil are called long oil varnishes and those with less oil are called short oil varnishes.

Long Oil Varnishes

The large amount of oil used in long oil varnishes makes them very tough and elastic. Exterior, spar, and marine spar varnishes are all long oil varnishes. They dry slowly and produce only a moderate gloss. Long oil varnishes should be used whenever weather resistance is the prime consideration. Long oil varnishes are not well suited for fine furniture because they can't be rubbed or polished and their long drying time makes it more likely that dust will be trapped in the finish.

Medium Oil Varnishes

When a durable interior finish is needed that has more gloss than a long oil finish, a medium oil varnish is used. Sometimes called cabinet varnish, medium oil varnish is probably the most versatile type because it can be used on a variety of projects. Varnishes of this type can be rubbed with pumice and rottenstone; however, the finish achieved by rubbing won't be as fine as a short oil varnish would produce.

Short Oil Varnishes

When a rubbed finish is desired, the best results are achieved when a short oil varnish is used. Short oil varnishes are strictly for interior use and are primarily used on fine furniture that won't receive rough handling. The finish produced by a short oil varnish is hard and somewhat brittle. The extreme hardness is the property that allows this type to take such a fine rubbed finish. Short oil

Illus. 103. Apply penetrating oil finish to the scratch and use wet-or-dry sandpaper to sand out the defect.

Illus. 104. After the finish is dry, no trace of the scratch is left.

varnishes are commonly called rubbing varnish, polishing varnish, or piano varnish.

Synthetic Varnishes

Synthetic varnishes have surpassed the natural varnishes in sales volume. This is because they are easier to use, more durable, and more versatile. In addition, they are faster drying, so there is less chance of dust accumulating on the wet surface.

The most popular synthetics are alkyd, polyurethane, and phenolic. Alkyd is the least expensive and is found in bargain brand varnishes. It is satisfactory when a fine finish is not needed. Polyurethane is probably the most universal of the synthetics; it is used for interior as well as exterior work and produces a hard and durable finish. Phenolics are used in some exterior and marine grade finishes.

Water Emulsion Varnish

Because of an increasing awareness of the health and safety problems that are posed by volatile solvents and because of the desirability of water cleanup, water emulsion varnishes have been developed. Though they are commonly called latex varnish, they don't actually contain latex. Early attempts at a water-based varnish weren't too successful; the finish was rough and always remained a bit tacky. But new advances have made water-based varnishes acceptable for a large number of uses. At present they are still not suitable for use on fine furniture, but they make the job of varnishing woodwork, household cabinets and everyday furniture much easier. They are applied much the same as any other varnish. Some may tend to raise the grain; if this is the case, treat the wood as was described for water-based stains. In most cases, the newer formulations don't raise the grain; check the product directions to make sure. Some varieties appear milky white when wet, but they dry clear.

Applying Varnish

Brushing is the usual method of application for varnish. You can spray varnish; usually it must be thinned with turpentine or paint thinner before spraying. Some varnishes will react with paste filler, turning the filler grey. Some stains will bleed through varnish. To solve either problem, you may want to consider using a sealer before varnishing. A thin coat of shellac will act as a good sealer for interior use under natural varnish, but don't use shellac under polyurethane because they are not compatible. Shellac should not be used for exterior applications because the moisture will affect the finish. Sanding sealer made specifically for the purpose will usually do a better job than shellac and provide a more water-resistant finish. For many varnishes, the recommended sealer is the varnish itself thinned 50 percent. This type of sealer will seal the wood's pores, but it won't prevent reactions between filler or stain and the varnish.

Always varnish in a well-ventilated area that is relatively dust-free. Because varnish dries so slowly, dust is a major problem. Damp mopping the floor just before varnishing will help to keep the dust down. Wipe the surface to be varnished with a tack rag to remove as much dust as possible.

Gloss varnish should not be stirred, as this only introduces air bubbles. Satin varnish contains a flattening agent that will settle to the bottom of the can, so you must stir satin varnish; but do it slowly and try to avoid whipping air into the varnish. Whether you intend to use satin or gloss as the final coat, you should apply gloss varnish as the first coat. The flattening agent in satin varnish will produce a cloudy finish that obscures the grain, if too many coats of it are applied; so satin varnish should be used for the last coat only.

Use a good varnish brush that is large enough to cover the surface with the minimum of brush strokes. Dip the brush into the varnish about half way. Press the brush against the inside of the can to remove the excess without creating air bubbles. Flow on the varnish by using the brush fairly full of varnish and refilling it before it becomes dry. After you have covered the surface with varnish in this manner, go over the same area with the brush without filling the brush with varnish. This brushing out will smooth and even out the varnish. Sometimes it is recommended that the varnish be flowed on with the grain, then brushed out across the grain followed by brushing out with the grain. It is said that this will force the varnish deeper into the pores of the wood; however, if this method is not done carefully, the resulting finish may have a checkerboard look. Usually it is better to do all brushing with the grain. Any resulting brush marks are much less noticeable.

The technique of applying varnish differs from that of many other finishes in that a heavy coat is desirable. A heavy coat of varnish will level itself, creating a smooth surface. If the coat is too thin, brush marks and laps will show more readily. However, too thick a coat will produce runs and drips, and it will dry too slowly; so try to apply just the right amount to get the varnish to level.

Whenever possible, position the work so that the surface being varnished will be horizontal. This allows you to apply a heavier coat that will level itself better without fear of runs or drips. Work with only one surface at a time, completely brushing out the area before moving to the next surface.

Follow the directions closely regarding the time between coats. Natural varnishes usually require 24 hours or more between coats, depending on the humidity. Some synthetics allow a period of several hours before a second coat can be added without sanding the first coat. But be careful. Applying the second coat too soon can produce a cloudy finish. If the time allowed has been exceeded,

then you must wait until the first coat is completely dry and lightly sand the surface before an additional coat can be applied. This is because the synthetics dry so hard that unless the second coat is applied while the first is still tacky or has been roughened with sandpaper, the second coat won't adhere to the first. Sanding between coats is a good idea anyway, because it allows you to sand out dust nibs that mar the surface and to flatten out any brush marks. Use 180 or finer sandpaper to sand between coats. Wet-or-dry sandpaper can be used with water as a lubricant to prevent the varnish from gumming up the sandpaper. Apply the water sparingly to avoid having it run into joints and swelling the wood. The best way is to use a damp sponge or rag; wipe it across the surface and then sand the area. Occasionally dip the sandpaper into a pan of water to wash it off. Wipe the accumulated paste from the work with a sponge or rag. When sanding is complete, wipe all of the remaining sanding residue from the surface and let it dry. Wipe the dry surface with a tack cloth to remove the last traces of dust and then apply the next coat. Two coats are sufficient for most ordinary work, but more coats can be used when you wish.

When the final coat is dry, it may be left as is or you can use pumice and rottenstone to create a rubbed finish.

Varnishing Problems

Modern varnishes are quite foolproof and will produce acceptable results even when they are applied improperly, but there are still problems that occur.

Fish eyes and crawling: When the surface that the varnish is applied to has a greasy or oily substance on it, the varnish won't adhere well. When the area is small, a round depression, called a fish eye, is formed. If the area is large, the problem is referred to as crawling. The best solution to this problem is to prevent its occurrence. Keep anything that contains grease, oil or silicones away from the surface to be finished. This problem is most prevalent when varnishing previously finished surfaces. Furniture wax and many household products contain silicones and other substances that will cause this problem. Some strippers contain wax that can also affect the adhesion of the final finish if they are not removed. When you suspect that the work may be contaminated by one of these substances, wash the surface with lacquer thinner or with a special silicone remover sold for this purpose.

Fish eyes and crawls are very hard to repair once they occur; if they cover a large area, the best bet is to remove the varnish with a rag soaked with thinner before the varnish is completely dry and start over. Small fish eyes can be sanded out but large ones will leave a noticeable depression if they are sanded out.

Rough texture: A rough surface texture can result if dust is allowed to settle on the varnish before it is dry. Dust in the surface is very easy to recognize; the rest of the surface will be smooth and glossy, but where the dust has landed there will be a small pointed bump. Sometimes the dust fibre will extend out of the top of the bump like a small hair. These dust nibs can be sanded out and will not affect the next coat, if they are sanded completely level with the surrounding surface. As you sand a dust nib, you will notice that they are usually surrounded by a circular area that is depressed below the surrounding area. This is because the dust acts as a wick conducting material from around the dust fibre up to a point. This makes thoroughly sanding out a dust nib a little more difficult, because the entire area must be sanded down to the low point of the depression.

A rough surface can also result when the wood was not thoroughly sanded beforehand. Varnishing causes preexisting defects to become more apparent.

Using old varnish that has skinned over or has a lot of material that has settled to the bottom can also create a rough surface.

If the varnish is applied too sparingly and brushed excessively, the surface will show brush marks and lap marks that didn't level themselves.

Runs and sags are caused by applying the varnish too heavily to a vertical surface. The surface tension of the varnish cannot hold it against the force of gravity. If you notice a run or sag while the varnish is still wet, brush it out. If you don't notice the run until after the varnish has become tacky, you may be able to remove it with a rag damp with thinner; then brush a little fresh varnish over the area. Runs that have dried must be sanded out.

Wrinkling is another problem that is caused by applying too much varnish in one coat. It is most likely to occur in corners and joints where the varnish from two adjoining surfaces runs together. The varnish is so thick in these areas that the top skins over before the varnish below has a chance to dry. As the varnish below does eventually dry, it contracts, causing wrinkles in the skin that formed first. To prevent wrinkling, brush out any area that may accumulate an excess of varnish. Once wrinkling occurs, let the varnish thoroughly dry and sand out the wrinkles. The wrinkled area will take much longer to dry than normal because the varnish is so thick. If it is not completely dry when it is sanded, the varnish will roll up into gummy balls and pull away from the surface, creating a depression.

LACQUER

Lacquer is the professional's first choice as a finishing coat. Practically all factory-built furniture receives a lacquer finish. Lacquer is hard and abrasion-resistant; it wears well and doesn't break down with age; it is resistant to water, alcohol, carbonated drinks,

Illus. 105. Lacquer is the finish most preferred for industrial application. Here automated spray equipment gives these chairs a fine lacquer finish.

absolutely can't spray it, then use a brushing lacquer; but if at all possible, apply lacquer by spraying.

Modern lacquers are entirely synthetic and contain none of the natural substance "lac" that is found in shellac. Modern lacquers began to be developed soon after World War I as a by-product of the explosives industry that had suffered a massive decline in production because of the end of the war. The word lacquer had been in use for many years before modern lacquer was developed, but it was used to describe a variety of finishes that bear no relation to today's lacquer.

The solvents used in lacquer will dissolve almost any other finish; for this reason lacquer is said to be "hotter" than other finishes. A "hot" finish like lacquer should not be applied over a "colder" finish such as varnish. If you apply a "hot" finish over a "cold" finish, the "hot" finish will dissolve the "cold" finish and the project will be ruined. On the other hand a "cold" finish can be successfully applied over a "hot" one. That is why shellac or lacquer can be used as a sealer under varnish.

Applying Lacquer

Lacquer produces a very thin layer per coat, so many coats are needed to finish the surface. Since lacquer dries rapidly, several coats can be applied on one day; so even though many coats are necessary, the finishing process is usually completed in less time than is needed for other finishes. Because many coats are needed, it is sometimes advantageous to use a lacquer sanding sealer as the first coat. Sanding sealer has solids added to the formula that help to fill the wood and build finish thickness. After the sealer has dried, it is sanded to provide a smooth surface for subsequent coats of lacquer. The addition of solids to sanding sealer makes them less transparent than lacquer and alters the color a little. The effect is only slight and usually of no consequence; but if

heat, and mild alkalis and acids. Unlike almost all other finishes, it is completely clear with no color of its own to alter the color of the wood or stain.

Lacquer dries rapidly and several coats can be applied in one day. The surface hardness of lacquer makes it ideal for rubbing with pumice and rottenstone or steel wool. Lacquer is well suited to application by automated equipment. (Illus. 105)

The only major disadvantage of lacquer is that, since it is a professional product, it takes professional equipment to apply it. Lacquer must be applied with spray equipment. There are some brushing lacquers available that contain a retarder to slow down the drying, but they really don't level as well as varnish. If you need to use lacquer and optimum clarity is desired, use lacquer without a sanding sealer.

Before spraying lacquer, it should be thinned about 25 percent with a quality thinner designed specifically for the purpose. The exact amount of thinner should be determined by experimentation and will vary depending on the application. If the air humidity exceeds 50 percent, about one-third of the thinner should be replaced by retarder; otherwise the lacquer may absorb moisture from the air and become slightly cloudy. This condition is called blushing.

When spraying lacquer with air-operated equipment, begin by setting the air pressure at 40 PSI and vary it up or down from that setting until optimum performance is achieved. Refer to Chapter 2 for specific instructions on how to use spray equipment.

Unlike varnish, each coat of lacquer will slightly dissolve the preceding coat, providing an excellent bond between coats; so sanding to provide a mechanical bond between coats is not necessary. However, you can sand between coats to remove dust and imperfections in the surface. Unless you are working in an extremely dusty location, dust won't be a problem with lacquer; it drys so fast the dust doesn't have time to settle.

Don't try for a heavy coat of lacquer; build the finish with many thin coats.

SHELLAC

Shellac is one of the oldest finishes still in use today. Most of the beautiful antiques you see in museums use some form of shellac to produce the classic finish that is so admired. Shellac is a resinous substance that is made from the secretions of a small insect called the lac bug (*tachardia lacca*). Most shellac comes from India where it is gathered by hand from deposits left by the lac bug in plum trees. It is processed and refined into several grades of dry flakes that produce liquid shellac when dissolved in alcohol.

Shellac is a very desirable finishing material because it is easy to apply, dries quickly and forms a flexible and elastic top coat that is very durable and able to withstand the rigors of time, as shown by the condition of finishes on antiques several hundred years old. However, shellac does have some disadvantages. Two major drawbacks are the fact that it is not very water resistant (water left on the surface will cause a white milky spot), and alcohol will dissolve it; so shellac should not be used for table tops or bar tops where spilled drinks are likely. Another disadvantage is a limited shelf life compared to other finishing materials.

Shellac is available in several types representing different degrees of refinement. Raw shellac is a dark orangish brown color; refining the shellac removes this color. But the refining process also decreases the shelf life of the shellac, so the more refined the shellac, the shorter its shelf life. The highly refined forms of shellac also seem to be less durable than the less refined grades.

Button shellac is the least refined grade of shellac available today. It gets its name from the fact that the flakes slightly resemble dark brown buttons. This grade has a very long shelf life; the flakes can be stored for years without deteriorating. The dark brown color of button shellac makes is suitable for use only when a very dark color is desired for the final finish. It is mainly used to duplicate antique finishes.

Orange shellac is a more refined grade of shellac, but it still retains some of the orangish brown color of the raw shellac. It also has a relatively long shelf life. Orange shellac is used for dark-colored finishes, as is button shellac; but because it is a light shade, more of the underlying color of the wood shows through.

Blonde shellac is light amber in color. It can be used for all but the highest finishes without imparting any noticeable change in the color of the finish.

White shellac is almost completely clear. It is produced by bleaching all of the color out of the shellac. When a very light-colored finish is desired, white shellac must be used; but if it is not necessary to use white shellac, blonde shellac will probably give better results. The bleaching process makes white shellac less durable, and white shellac has the shortest shelf life of any type of shellac.

When purchasing white shellac, always check the expiration date stamped on the container. Only purchase the amount of white shellac that you need for the job at hand and use the product promptly. White shellac flakes only have a shelf life of two to three months after which they won't dissolve properly, so white shellac is almost exclusively sold in liquid form. The liquid has a shelf life of about one year, but because some of that time has expired before you buy the product, you should use the shellac within a month of purchase. White shellac that has gone out of date won't dry properly. It will remain gummy and never harden. If you want to use shellac that has gone past its expiration date, always test it on a scrap to make sure it will dry; if it does, it is safe to use. The expiration dates printed on the container are usually conservative, so it is often all right to use the product for several months past the date if you test it before use.

There are two other grades of shellac that aren't as commonly available but are still made by some manufacturers. Garnet shellac is more refined than button shellac, but retains more of the brown color than orange shellac does. Beta shellac is lighter than orange shellac, but not as light as blonde.

Mixing Shellac

Except for white shellac, the shellac flakes have a longer shelf life than the liquid shellac, so it is best to buy the flakes and then mix a fresh batch of liquid shellac just before use. To make liquid shellac, the flakes are dissolved in alcohol. The best type of alcohol to use is ethyl alcohol; this is the same type of alcohol found in liquor However, water mixed with the alcohol will harm the shellac, so only alcohol designated as a solvent should be used. Methanol, or wood alcohol, tends to make the shellac brittle or gummy and should not be used to dissolve the flakes. By law, ethyl alcohol has to be made undrinkable to be sold as a solvent; to do this, small amounts of poisonous substances such as wood alcohol or gasoline must be added to the alcohol. Ethyl alcohol that has been treated in this manner is called denatured alcohol or proprietory solvent. It's best to stick with a high quality solvent for shellac, because too much wood alcohol in the mix will degrade the quality of the shellac.

Liquid shellac is categorized by the amount of dry flakes used in relation to the amount of solvent. This is referred to as the "cut." If one pound of flakes is dissolved into one gallon of solvent, a one-pound cut is produced. Typically, shellac is mixed as a four-pound cut (four pounds of flakes to one gallon of solvent) and then thinned at the time of application to a two- or three-pound cut. Usually only a pint or quart of liquid is mixed at one time.

To make one quart of four-pound cut shellac, put 12 ounces of shellac flakes in a glass container and pour three cups of alcohol over the flakes. Put the lid on the container and let the flakes dissolve. You can speed up the process by occasionally shaking the container. When the flakes are thoroughly dissolved, strain the shellac through several layers of cheesecloth or a commercial paint strainer.

Before using the shellac, you will need to add additional alcohol to thin the shellac to the required cut. The first coat of shellac should be thinned to a one-pound cut; subsequent coats can be a one- or two pound cut. Sometimes a three-pound cut is used for the final coat. To dilute four-pound cut shellac to three-pound cut, add one-half pint of alcohol to a quart of four-pound cut shellac. To make a two-pound cut shellac, add three-fourths quart of alcohol to a quart of four-pound cut shellac. One pound-cut shellac requires two quarts of alcohol added to one quart of four-pound cut shellac. You can see that if you follow these proportions exactly, you may end up with a lot more shellac than you need. For example, you will end up with three quarts of one-pound cut shellac. Most finishers dilute shellac in smaller quantities and add the alcohol until the shellac seems the right consistency. Once you become familiar with the various cuts, this is easy to do and allows you to slightly vary the consistency to fit the job at hand. Some finishers rub the shellac between their thumb and forefinger to judge the cut. It takes judgment and experience to accurately thin shellac by feel, so at first measure the amount of alcohol you add. You can scale down the amounts as long as you keep the proportions the same as shown above.

Applying Shellac

Shellac can be applied with a brush, a sprayer, or with a pad. When shellac is applied with a pad, the technique is called French polishing.

The alcohol used to dissolve the shellac has an affinity for water and will absorb water from a damp surface or from humid air. So, shellac should never be applied to a damp surface or when the air humidity is especially high. If water is allowed to combine with the shellac, the resulting finish will have a milky white appearance. Shellac cannot be applied over fresh stain; the stain should be allowed to dry for 24 hours before shellac is applied.

Brushing shellac.   To brush shellac, thin it to a one-pound cut for the first coat. Use a good quality natural filament brush. Because shellac dries so quickly, the material must be applied and brushed out in one operation. Apply the shellac to the wood in one long uniform stroke, then immediately brush over the area again to smooth out the coating. Apply more shellac to the next area, slightly overlapping the first stroke. Don't try to make a brushful go too far; refill the brush as soon as it shows signs of becoming dry.

Once you have covered an area, don't go back to brush it out again; the shellac will already be partially set, and prominent brush marks will be left. The secret to successfully brushing shellac is to work quickly. The shellac remains liquid on the surface of the wood for only a short time; once it has begun to gel, any further brushing will degrade the finish.

After the first coat has dried thoroughly (at least four hours), sand the surface with 320 grit sandpaper to remove any dust nibs. Shellac has a tendency to gum up sandpaper, so use open coat or non-clog paper. As soon as a spot of gummed up shellac begins to appear on the sandpaper, remove it with your fingernail or a pocketknife. Only a light sanding is necessary to remove dust nibs; each coat of shellac will weld itself to the previous one, so it is not necessary to rough up the surface to ensure good adhesion. If you want to build up the coating fast, switch to a two-pound cut for the next coat and finish with a three-pound cut for the final coat. But for the best finish, stay with a one-pound cut and apply five or more coats. Allow at least four hours between coats, and sand between coats if the surface appears rough.

Spraying shellac.   Shellac can also be applied with a spray gun. Thin the shellac to at least a two-pound cut. A small syphon-feed gun can easily handle shellac. Keep air pressure low, 30 PSI maximum. The distance from the work is more critical with shellac than when spraying other finishes; if it is too close, runs and sags develop quickly. Holding the gun too far away will result in a rough sandpaper texture. The proper distance is approximately six inches, but this will vary some depending on the air pressure used and the cut of the shellac.

French polishing. French polishing is a traditional method of applying shellac that uses a cloth pad to apply the finish. French polishing produces the best possible finish from shellac, but it requires a lot of skill, labor, and patience to apply a French polish. Before the advent of modern lacquers and spray equipment, French polishing was widely used for fine furniture; but the time and skilled labor needed to produce a French polish finish have virtually eliminated it as a method of commercial finishing. However, do-it-yourselfers and custom craftsmen who are interested in duplicating antique finishes still practice the ancient art of French polishing. Today it is used mostly on small items such as jewelry boxes or on the most expensive antique reproductions.

In its purest state, French polishing is done on wood that has no filler applied; but if you want to take short cuts, you can skip the process of filling the pores with French polish by applying a paste wood filler first. If you use paste filler, let it dry thoroughly, then brush on a thin coat of shellac. When the shellac is thoroughly dry, sand it with 400 grit sandpaper until it is perfectly smooth. If the wood is to be stained, use only water stain because the polishing process will rub off most other stains.

French polishing should be done in a warm dry room. The temperature should be at least 68°F (20°C) and the air humidity should be relatively low.

Making the pad. The first thing you need to apply a French polish is a set of pads. The pads are made from balls of lamb's wool, wool yarn cut up into small lengths, cotton balls, or wadded-up rags. The balls should be about two inches in diameter. Cover the balls with a piece of close-weave cotton or linen fabric. Gather the fabric together on one side of the ball and secure it by tying thread around the gathered edges of the cloth. Make three or more of these pads at once. Each pad is used in a separate step, and if it is kept in a tightly capped, air-tight container it will last for a long time.

Grip the pad like you would a baseball with the gathered edges inside your palm. In use, the pad will develop a flat side where it contacts the work and the pad will comfortably conform to your hand.

In all steps of French polishing, the pad should be filled by pouring the shellac on the back of the pad near the neck of gathered material. Don't pour the liquid on the face of the pad or dip the pad into the liquid. The pad should just be damp, never dripping wet. After filling the pad, distribute the liquid evenly throughout by pressing the pad against the palm of your hand or a clean piece of cardboard.

Filling. The first step in traditional French polishing is filling. If you have elected to use a paste wood filler, this step can be skipped. Choose a pad to be used exclusively for filling. Thin some one-pound cut shellac until it is almost as thin as the alcohol itself. Fill the pad with this thinned shellac. Rub the pad over the surface of the wood using a circular motion. Occasionally add a little thinned shellac to the back of the pad. Sprinkle a little fine pumice on the surface as you continue to rub the pad over the wood. The pumice will grind off fine wood dust as you rub; the combination of the wood dust and the pumice mixed with the shellac will be forced into the pores of the wood, filling them. Because dust from the wood itself is mixed with the filler, the color will match the surrounding wood closely. Con-

Illus. 106. To fill the pores of open-grained woods with the French polishing process, sprinkle pumice on the surface and rub with a pad that has been filled with very thin shellac.

Illus. 107. To build up a film of French polish, switch to a new pad and fill it with one-pound cut shellac. Sprinkle a few drops of oil on the surface to lubricate the pad.

tinue this process until all of the pores are filled. (Illus. 106)

Building up a film. Once the pores are filled, allow the filler at least 12 hours to dry before proceeding. Change to a new pad to be used for building up a film of shellac on the surface. This pad is filled with one-pound cut shellac. Sprinkle a few drops of mineral oil or raw linseed oil on the surface of the wood to lubricate the motion of the pad. Work in quick circular strokes and keep the pad in constant motion. (Illus. 107) If the pad is left stationary on the surface even for an instant, it will stick and mar the work. Feed the pad from the back with more shellac as the pad dries out. After the surface has been coated in this manner, let the shellac dry about 12 hours before applying another coat. About four coats are needed to achieve a high gloss finish.

Spiriting off. Once you have achieved the surface buildup you are after, one final step remains. The oil used to lubricate the pad needs to be removed from the surface. This process is called spiriting off. Allow the last coat to dry for at least 24 hours. Change to a new pad and fill it with alcohol only; the pad should feel almost dry to the touch. As you progress, use less and less alcohol until you are using a pad that is almost completely dry at the last. Rub the pad with the grain across the surface of the work to remove the oil. (Illus. 108) Use very light pressure; don't go over one area too much or you will soften the finish. Let the finish "rest" for about one hour, then go back and touch up any oily looking spots. This process should produce the characteristic sheen of a French polish finish. (Illus. 109)

Although the steps involved sound relatively simple, the process is difficult to master because a lot of it depends on touch and judgment that can only be gained through practice. If you are willing to invest the time it takes to learn this art, you will be rewarded with beautiful finishes that everyone will envy.

Another form of French polishing is called open pore French polishing. This type produces a satin finish that shows all of the texture of the pores.

To produce an open pore finish, the pad is

92

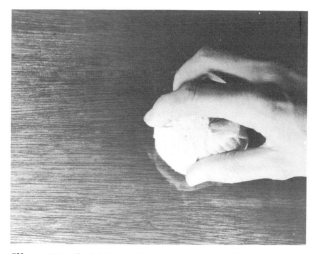

Illus. 108. Spiriting off removes the oil left on the surface. Use a clean pad moistened with alcohol.

Illus. 109. The French polishing process produces a fine finish with a deep lustre.

fed with one-pound cut shellac and the pad is always moved with the grain. No oil or pumice is necessary, and it is not necessary to spirit off the work at the end.

TWO-PART FINISHES

When certain resins are mixed with a catalyst or hardener, they harden chemically by a process called polymerization. These resins are useful as wood finishes, because once they are catalyzed, they are extremely hard and resist acids, alcohol, and most common solvents. Since they harden by a chemical reaction that takes place evenly throughout the film thickness, it is possible to apply very thick coats of the finish. Such a thick coat would be impractical with a finish that relies on evaporation of solvents to dry, because the top layer would dry before the inside of the film thickness could dry. Also, since no evaporation takes place in a catalyzed finish, there is no shrinkage; so this type of finish will fill surface irregularities and defects.

The most common uses for two-part finishes are bar tops, table tops, and small decorative items where it is used to embed pictures, leaves, or other flat objects in the finish. (Illus. 110)

Two-part finishes can be brushed or sprayed, but the most common way to apply them is to pour. Pouring the finish onto a flat horizontal surface takes advantage of the fin-

Illus. 110. Two-part finishes are frequently used to embed objects on the surface of decorative plaques.

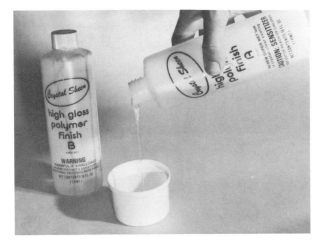

Illus. 111. To mix a two-part finish, pour equal parts of resin and hardener into a disposable container.

Illus. 112. Stir the resin and hardener together with a flat-bottomed stick. Frequently scrape the bottom and sides of the container to get any unmixed materials that may be there.

ish's ability to flow out level and fill minor defects. It's also the best way to achieve the extremely thick look of this type of finish.

The two parts of the finish should be mixed just prior to use, and only as much as you can apply in about half an hour should be made at one time. Follow the directions on the container for exact mixing instructions; usually you mix equal parts of hardener with resin. (Illus. 111) It's best to use a disposable container to mix the resin in, because it is very difficult to clean up. But don't use a waxed paper cup; the wax may contaminate the finish. If you use a paper cup, use the unwaxed kind. A tin can makes a good mixing container as long as it has been washed out thoroughly. Use a flat wooden stick to stir the mixture; a tongue depressor is just the right size, but its round end makes it difficult to scrape the bottom of the container. You can make a supply of mixing sticks by setting a table saw rip fence to make a ⅛-in. strip and sawing several strips off the edge of a ¾-in.-thick board. Thorough mixing is of extreme importance. Work quickly, and frequently scrape the sides and bottom of the container to make sure that no pockets of unmixed resin remain there. (Illus. 112)

Small items should be suspended on wood blocks or by nails driven into the bottom so that the resin that drips off the edge won't seep under the object and glue it to the work surface.

To apply the resin to a small object, simply pour it into the center of the surface and let it flow over the entire surface. (Illus. 113) For larger surfaces, you will have to pour the resin in several areas; and it may be necessary to use a strip of cardboard to spread it out. If you have to do any spreading, work quickly before the resin starts to set so there will be time for the resin to flow out level. Once the resin starts to gel, it will form ridges and dips that will not flow out. Knotholes and other defects can be filled by pouring additional resin into them. If the defect goes all the way through the board, cover the underside of the hole with masking tape to prevent the resin from seeping out the bottom.

If bubbles appear in the surface, blow on them to break them and they will flow out. If the resin has begun to set before you notice a bubble, you can still remove it by blowing hot air from a hair dryer at it. The hot air will break the bubble and make the resin fluid

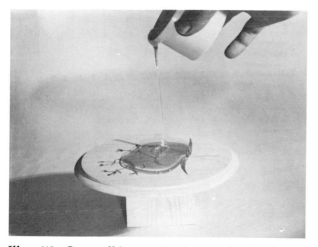

Illus. 113. On small items, simply pour the finish onto the center of the object. The finish will naturally flow over the entire surface and level itself.

enough to flow out and hide the depression left by the bubble. The hair dryer can also be used to help ridges and spreading marks flow out. This trick will only work in the early stages of setting; after a while the heat will only serve to speed up the setting process and further harden the resin.

If additional coats are necessary, follow the manufacturer's directions closely; some types may be recoated without sanding if it is done within a certain time limit. After the time limit has expired, the resin must be allowed to completely cure and then the surface sanded to make a good mechanical bond.

If you don't want the thick look achieved by pouring, you can brush the resin on. The finish achieved will look about like ordinary varnish, but it will have the extra strength of a catalyzed finish. Brushes must be cleaned thoroughly in the recommended solvent (usually acetone) before the resin sets or you will have to throw them away, because conventional solvents won't dissolve the finish once it has set.

Two-part finishes can also be sprayed. Standard two-part finishes can be thinned with the proper solvent, or finishes especially formulated for spraying can be used.

In either case be sure to thoroughly clean the gun before the resin sets or the gun will be ruined.

PAINT

Paint is one of the oldest protective coatings. It was probably first used more for its decorative qualities and that is still the case in many instances, but ancient people soon discovered that paint could protect a surface as well as decorate it. The Barrier Canyon Indians who lived in what is now southeastern Utah around 4500 B.C. used paint to make giant illustrations called pictographs on the face of sandstone cliffs. Many pictographs survive today, attesting to the durability of paint. But even though paint has such ancient origins, in the last few decades it has probably changed more than any other finishing product. In fact, the paint industry is undergoing what could be termed a revolution.

Terminology is a major casualty of this revolution. In an effort to avoid confusing the public, paint manufacturers have applied traditional paint names to new products, but in some ways this has only added to the confusion. For example, at one time almost all quality paints were made with linseed oil. They were called oil-based paint. Today linseed oil has largely been replaced by other ingredients, but the name oil-based paint is still applied to new products. Until recently oil-based meant that the product had to be thinned and cleaned up with mineral spirits, but now there are some oil-based products that can be cleaned up with water.

Latex is another term that has changed its meaning over the past few years. It is a type of rubber that was used in the early water clean-up paints. The name latex stayed with water clean-up paints even though now they usually contain synthetic plastics like acrylic resins. Gradually the name latex came to mean any water clean-up paint, but now that distinction is blurred by the introduction of water clean-up oil-based paints.

Enamel is another paint term that has lost its original meaning. This was originally a single product that was made by adding colored pigments to varnish. The resulting paint was prized for its glasslike surface, toughness, and washability. At present the term enamel is applied to a wide variety of paint products of varying composition. Generally it means that the paint is more durable or washable than other paints.

Because paint has been in use for so long there is a lot of folklore associated with it. The paint revolution has made practically all of the old folk formulas and methods of manufacture obsolete. There are dozens of old formulas for paint fortifiers that use linseed oil, white lead, turpentine and other ingredients. Don't use any of them. Modern paints are superior. You should also realize that they are made to be used straight from the can. The addition of any unapproved ingredients will degrade or ruin the paint.

An obsolete piece of folk wisdom about paint is that you can judge a paint's quality by how heavy the can feels. This is based on the fact that lead was a major ingredient of most paint formulas. More lead in the paint made it feel heavier, and therefore it was supposedly better quality. Since lead has been found to be a health hazard when used in paint, it is no longer included in paint formulas, so the weight of paint has nothing to do with its quality.

Today the only reliable source of information about a specific type of paint is the label on the can or literature provided by the manufacturer. Most paint cans have a list of ingredients on the label. By analyzing the ingredients you can get a better idea of what you are getting. The label will usually list the following basic categories of ingredients: pigments, extenders, resins, oils, and solvents. Resins, oils and solvents together are known as the "vehicle."

Pigments

Pigments are finely ground minerals or synthetic materials that give the paint its color. Some of the natural mineral pigments are similar to the pigments used thousands of years ago. Others have been developed very recently. The degree of fineness to which the pigments are ground plays a role in how smooth the resulting finish will be. The paints using the coarsest pigments are called barn paints. They are especially well suited for rough lumber. House paints use finer pigments. The most finely ground pigments are used in interior paints formulated for use on furniture and woodwork.

Besides providing the color of the paint, pigments play a role in the hiding power of the paint and in the paint's durability. White pigments are used in all but the darkest colors of paint because some of the white pigments offer more hiding power than any other type.

White Lead. In the past white lead was one of the most widely used paint pigments, but lead is poisonous and will cause serious health problems when its dust is inhaled or when particles are eaten. This is particularly a problem for young children because they have a tendency to eat chips of paint that peel from the surface. For this reason, the United States government has banned lead compounds from most paint products. You need to be careful when you are working on a surface that you suspect was previously painted with a paint that has a high lead content (nearly all paint manufactured prior to 1950 contains lead). Wear a dust mask or respirator to avoid inhaling particles of the paint. If you scrape loose paint from the surface, use a drop cloth to collect the chips and dispose of them in accordance with local dump regulations. Don't allow chips of lead paint to fall into the soil around a house while you are working on an exterior paint job. Plants grown in the soil will accumulate high concentrations of lead. This is particularly bad if the area is used as a vegetable garden.

Titanium Dioxide. Titanium dioxide is a fairly new pigment. It has a very high hiding power and is extremely durable. It has taken over as the most widely used pigment. Each of its many forms is designated by a roman numeral. The various types have different properties that make them suitable for different applications, but when choosing paint it is usually not important to know what type of titanium dioxide was used. What is important is how much was used. Titanium dioxide is one of the most expensive pigments, so inexpensive paints will skimp on it. Generally, the higher the amount of titanium dioxide, the higher the paint quality. However, as with almost everything in the rapidly changing paint industry, this is not a hard and fast rule. Very dark colors won't use any titanium dioxide because its white color would lighten the paint too much. A high concentration of titanium dioxide is more important in an exterior paint because it offers more durability. Interior paints may not need as much.

Lithopone. A white pigment that is frequently used in interior paint when the durability of titanium dioxide is not needed.

Zinc Oxide. Sometimes used in exterior paint to control mildew. It is not suitable for use in large proportions because it may cause the paint to crack, but in small quantities it can improve the paint's performance.

Colored Pigments. In most paints the colored pigments make up only a small volume of the total pigments in the paint. Most of the paint's properties come from the type of white pigment used. In very dark paints pigments like burnt umber, iron oxides, or carbon black may be substituted for the white pigment.

Extenders

Extenders are also called suspenders or fillers and are usually listed with the pigments on the paint-can label. Extenders are a necessary ingredient in all paints. They improve the paint's working characteristics and help suspend the pigments in the vehicle. However, when the extenders make up a large percentage of the total amount of pigments the quality of the paint will be lowered. Some common extenders are silica, calcium carbonate, barium sulfate, calcium sulfate, aluminum silicate, magnesium silicate, and mica. Mica and magnesium silicate help to reduce cracking of the dried paint film. Mica is also added to some acrylic latex paints to make them more water repellent.

Resins

Resins glue the pigments and extenders together to form the dry paint film. They are sometimes referred to as binders. In modern paints the type of resin used is one of the most important considerations. The resin used determines what the paint is suitable for and how durable it will be.

Acrylic. Acrylic resin, a synthetic plastic, is one of the most popular resins for use in water-based paints. It produces a tough water repellent film that adheres well to wood. Acrylic latex paints have two properties that make them very desirable as a wood finish. The paint film will keep out liquid water, but it will allow water vapor to pass through it. This property is called breathability. Paints that breathe allow the wood to adapt to climatic changes without causing paint blisters. Acrylic paints are also very flexible, so the wood can expand and contract without cracking the paint film.

Alkyd. Alkyd resin is also a synthetic resin. Almost all modern oil-based paints contain alkyd resin. Alkyd can also be used in water-based paints, usually in connection with another resin such as acrylic. Oil-based alkyds produce a very tough, long-lasting paint film that is impervious to water. This makes them ideal for use in wet locations to prevent water from damaging the wood, but because they don't breathe, they are more likely to blister if the wood has a high moisture content. Water-based alkyds produce a breathing film, so in that respect they are superior to the oil-based type for use on wood. An oil-based alkyd will adhere better to old, weathered paint, so it is sometimes preferred for repainting previously painted wood. However, the water-based type is constantly improving in this respect.

Polyurethane. Polyurethane resins are used in paints when an extremely tough abrasion-resistant film is needed. Polyurethane paint is much more expensive than alkyd or acrylic, but it will pay for itself through its durability in some situations. Polyurethane paints come in two types. The first comes as a single liquid just like most paint and can be handled like ordinary paint. The second type comes as two separate liquids. Once they are mixed together the paint will remain a liquid for about eight hours. After that it will harden into solid plastic even if it is in a sealed can. This type is tougher and more weather-resistant than the single liquid type.

Epoxy. Epoxy resin is similar to polyurethane resin, only it is even tougher. Epoxy won't produce quite as glossy a finish as polyurethane. Like polyurethane, it is available as a single liquid or as a two-part catalyzed finish.

Vinyl. When flexibility of the paint film is of prime importance, vinyl resins are used. Vinyl is used mostly in water-based paints, sometimes in conjunction with one of the other resins.

Butadiene-Styrene. This resin is one of the first types used to make latex paint. It is low cost and yet still gives a tough rubbery film.

A variety of other resins including polyethylene, polystyrene, polyester, and phenolics are also used, usually in connection with one of the other resins listed above. Each additional resin is included to add a specific quality to the paint such as durability, water resistance or washability.

Oils

Several types of oils are used in paint to add desirable qualities to the final film. They tend to make the paint film more durable and water resistant. They are desirable in paint that is used as a wood finish because they tend to soak into the wood and help preserve it. Although oils are mostly associated with oil-based paint, many water-based paints incorporate some oils into their formulas. Linseed oil was once used almost exclusively, but now a wide variety of other oils such as soya oil, tung oil, safflower oil, sunflower oil, and others are also used.

Solvents

So far all of the ingredients discussed have contributed in some way to the final paint film. The job of the solvents is different. They are meant to evaporate from the paint as it dries, leaving only the other ingredients behind. The solvents thin the paint to a workable consistency and make it easier to apply by helping it flow out to create a smooth surface.

By far the most popular solvent in use today is water because of its many advantages. It is inexpensive, makes cleanup easy, is non-flammable, is non-toxic, evaporates quickly, and it has no odor. The only major disadvantage of using water as a paint solvent is that it will inevitably raise the grain of bare wood.

Mineral spirits is another popular solvent. Most oil-based paints use mineral spirits or a similar product as the solvent. The main disadvantage of mineral spirits is that its fumes are toxic and flammable.

Some paints (epoxies and lacquers, for example) require special solvents such as acetone or methyl ethyl ketone that are very volatile.

When it is necessary to thin paint, the thinner should be compatible with the solvents in the paint. Always use the type of thinner recommended on the paint can.

Primers

Primers are necessary whenever you are painting bare wood. Top-coat paints don't penetrate deep into bare wood, so they don't adhere well to it. Primers are formulated to penetrate the wood, thus helping preserve it and holding the paint film firmly in place. They dry with a slightly rough surface that is called "tooth" which makes a better bond between the primer and the top coat. Paint folklore has it that you can make a good primer by thinning the top coat 50%. This is no longer valid. If you try this method, you risk having the paint peel or blister at a later date.

Each manufacturer markets what is called a "paint system" that consists of several paint products including primers, wall paint, exterior paint, and interior enamel, that are all compatible with each other. Once you have decided on a particular type of paint, stay with that system for all of the other products you will use on the job. That way you can be sure there won't be any problems of incompatibility between the products.

Most systems offer at least two types of primers for use on bare wood. One is usually an oil-based alkyd and the other is water-based. Water-based products will raise the grain of bare wood so you should use the oil-based primer on surfaces such as interior woodwork or cabinets that need a smooth surface. For building exteriors, raised grain doesn't present as much of a problem because some wood texture is usually desirable aesthetically. So, if you can tolerate the raised grain, a water-based primer will perform better for exterior use because it produces a breathing film while the oil-based primer produces an impervious film. If you use an oil-based primer under a paint like acrylic latex, you lose some of the advantage gained by choosing the breathing paint because the primer won't breathe.

Some types of wood contain pigments that will bleed through a paint film, creating a stain on the finished surface. Woods that are especially prone to bleeding are redwood, cedar, mahogany, and fir. Knots in other types of wood, especially pine, are very prone to bleeding. Bleeding stains can appear even after the paint has been dry for several months. Follow the recommendations on the paint can for handling bleeding problems. It will recommend one of the products in the same system that contains a sealer to prevent bleed-through. It may be one of the primers or it may be a separate sealer.

One product that is often recommended as a sealer is pigmented shellac. It is similar to the shellac discussed earlier, but a high hiding pigment such as titanium dioxide has been added. Usually pigmented shellac is an alcohol-based product like the other forms of shellac, but a new development is a water-based product called pigmented latex shellac. This product combines non-volatile shellac with acrylic resin and titanium dioxide. It can be used as a primer and sealer.

What Woods to Paint

Choosing the type of wood you will apply paint to is as important as choosing the type of paint. The underlying wood plays an important role in how the final finish looks and how durable it is.

For exterior use and for use in wet interior locations, redwood and cedar are the top choices. Even though they have bleeding problems, they can easily be sealed to prevent this. Paint adheres to these woods very well and, because they are so decay- and rot-resistant, there isn't any problem of deterioration under the paint film.

When interior trim such as door and window casing and baseboards are to be painted, they are usually made of pine or fir but other woods such as hemlock are also used. Finger joints joining several short pieces into one long piece of moulding are usually unacceptable if the woodwork is to be stained and given a clear finish, but they don't present a problem if the moulding will be painted—as long as the joints are well made so that no gaps are visible through the paint.

For strictly utilitarian interior cabinet work, fir plywood is acceptable, but it is not well suited for fine work where appearance is important because the grain absorbs paint so unevenly that there is almost always some grain that shows through the paint.

Birch plywood is an ideal choice for fine cabinetry and furniture that will be painted. Paint adheres well to its surface and it absorbs paint uniformly. It is close-grained so very little texture shows through the paint and its subtle grain doesn't affect the final appearance of the paint. Also, because of its light color, there is no problem with bleeding or with coverage when using light-colored paint.

The man-made wood products lend themselves well to a paint finish. One of the best is tempered hardboard. Its super-smooth surface will produce very good results when painted. Particle board is not as smooth as tempered hardboard, but the better grades have a smooth enough surface to accept a good finish. Some types of particle board are available with a preprimed face that accepts paint very well. Medium-density overlay plywood (MDO) and high-density overlay plywood (HDO) are specifically designed to be painted. They have a plywood core like most plywood, but the face veneer is a man-made product rather than a wood veneer. The surface of these plywoods is very smooth and has no grain. They are often used for exterior siding, and make a good substitute for birch plywood in interior cabinetwork.

All of the man-made wood products should be primed with an oil-based primer if the smoothest surface is needed. Water-based products will cause the particles of wood to swell, creating bumps. Many of these products come preprimed from the factory.

Specific Applications

There are some specific applications for which a particular paint product is best. For exterior wood siding, acrylic latex is the leading choice at present. Because it breathes and is flexible it doesn't blister, crack, or peel. Of course, this is only true when applying the paint to new work. No product will glue down an old paint film that has failed. If a previously painted surface has blisters or is cracking and peeling, the old paint must be removed from those areas and the underlying problem corrected.

For interior mouldings, a semi-gloss acrylic latex enamel is a good choice. But use an oil-based primer on bare wood.

The type of paint used on furniture depends on the type of finish desired. Pine or particle board unfinished furniture can be painted with semi-gloss acrylic latex enamel if an oil-based primer is used first. If the furniture will receive heavy use, consider polyurethane or epoxy. For fine furniture, lacquer is the best choice. Lacquer paint is similar to the clear lacquer discussed earlier. It possesses all of the qualities previously described and the pigments used are usually very finely ground to give the smoothest possible finish. You can rub out a lacquered surface with pumice and rottenstone, steel wool or rubbing compound. Lacquer is available in a wide range of colors. Black is frequently used to finish Oriental-style furniture. Lacquer should only be applied by spraying; it is available in spray cans for those who don't have spray equipment. Follow the can label closely regarding the use of primers because lacquer will lift most conventional primers. Some lacquers can be applied directly to bare wood. If you want to repaint a previously painted surface with lacquer, you may need to remove the old paint or apply a special sealer because lacquer is not compatible with most other kinds of paint. Lacquer is a professional product and is more difficult to apply than most paints, but it will provide the best-looking finish on fine furniture.

Floors are subject to a lot of wear and abrasion. If you want to paint a wood floor, use a paint specifically designated as a floor paint. In very high traffic areas, you may need to use a catalyzed polyurethane or epoxy to get the most durable finish.

Applying Paint

Paint can be applied with a brush, roller, pad applicator, or spray equipment. The technique of brushing paint depends on whether the paint is oil-based or water-based. Oil-based paint should be brushed out to a uniform thin coat by going over the same area several times, otherwise the paint film may be too thick and runs, sags or wrinkling may develop. Water-based paint, on the other hand, is very slippery and overbrushing will result in a coat that is too thin. Stop brushing an area as soon as you have achieved a smooth covering. Either natural or synthetic filament brushes can be used with oil-based paints, but only synthetic filaments should be used with water-based paints.

Rollers and pad applicators work well with either oil-based or water-based paint. Pad applicators are especially well suited for exterior clapboard siding. When applying paint to a large surface with a roller, roll over the same area in several random directions to prevent lap marks.

An important principle in painting is keeping a wet edge. Lap marks will occur if you don't observe this rule. Plan your work so that you can paint an entire surface in one step. This is more difficult on large surfaces like building exteriors, but you can usually find natural stopping places like doors, windows or corners. If you stop in the middle of a large wall and then resume painting after the paint has dried, there will be a noticeable line at the joint between the two applications of paint.

Spray equipment can be used to apply most types of paint. (See p. 57-68). Some will require thinning. Follow the manufacturer's recommendations about what type of thinner to use. Water-based paints usually are more difficult to spray than oil-based paints. You need a different type of nozzle to spray water-based paint with some sprayers. Airless spray equipment can handle thicker paints better than types that use compressed air.

Prepare new wood for painting as you would for any finish by sanding it if a smooth surface is desired. A rough surface is desirable for some types of exterior siding and in that case no special preparation is needed. When repainting an old surface, thoroughly wash the old paint to remove accumulations of grease, wax or dirt that may prevent the new paint from sticking. Flat paint can be painted over without sanding, but gloss paint should be deglossed by sanding with 150 grit sandpaper. Deglossing liquid is an alternative that slightly dissolves the top surface of the old paint and makes it dull.

Whenever you will need more than one can of paint to complete a job mix all of the paint together before starting the job. Mixing compensates for variations in color between the individual cans. You can avoid the messy job of mixing by buying paint in larger containers. Paint stores that cater to professionals usually sell paint in five gallon containers, and some do-it-yourself-oriented stores are beginning to do likewise.

Paint Problems

If you follow the directions closely when applying modern paint to new wood, you are unlikely to have any problems. But when you repaint a surface that was painted with one of the older types of paint, you may encounter some of the following problems.

Blistering.   Blistering is most likely to occur on building exteriors. (Illus 114) Moisture from inside the building (especially near bathrooms, laundry rooms and kitchens) travels through the walls because the sun heating the exterior of the wall draws moisture out. When the paint applied to the wall is of the non-breathing type (or there are too many layers of it), the moisture can't escape so pressure builds up behind the paint. Eventually the pressure loosens the bond be-

tween the paint and the wood and a blister forms. Modern buildings incorporate a vapor barrier in the wall construction to help solve this problem, but older buildings lack this feature. When repainting a blistered surface use a scraper to remove all of the blisters. Prime the bare wood below the blister with a breathing primer, then paint the area with a breathing paint like acrylic latex. Unless you remove all of the old paint from the surface, the blistering problem is likely to reoccur in the areas that weren't scraped. You may be able to reduce the chances of more blisters forming by installing small vents in the wall to let the moisture out. To be truly effective, the vents must be placed at the top and bottom of each stud cavity because fire bridging usually blocks the cavity in the middle.

Peeling and Flaking.   Like blistering, this problem may be caused by moisture, or it may be due to lack of flexibility in the old paint. (Illus. 115) Wood expands and con-

Illus. 114. Blistering.

Illus. 115. Peeling and flaking.

102

tracts with climatic changes. If the paint is not capable of flexing with the wood, it will crack and eventually flake off. To correct this problem, remove all of the loose paint and prime the bare wood before repainting.

If recently applied paint peels from an old surface it is probably because the old surface was not adequately prepared before repainting. Thoroughly wash the surface to remove grease or dirt that may prevent paint adhesion and degloss glossy paint by sanding or using a liquid deglosser.

Mildew. Mildew is a fungus that grows on moist surfaces. (Illus. 116) It is especially a problem in areas that have a climate with high temperatures and humidity, but it can occur in any climate if moisture is present on the paint film for long periods of time. Before repainting, thoroughly wash the mildew from the paint with a solution of one part liquid chlorine bleach mixed in three parts water. Tough spots may require a higher con-

centration of bleach. Rinse thoroughly with clear water. When repainting, choose a paint that contains a fungicide to prevent regrowth of the mildew.

Alligatoring. When the surface of the paint cracks and pulls apart in a pattern that looks like alligator skin, the problem is called alligatoring. (Illus. 117) This problem can occur with new paint if the primer was incompatible with the top coat. It can also occur when new paint is applied over a glossy surface without first deglossing the surface.

It also occurs when many layers of old paint dry out and become brittle. The only solution is to remove the old paint.

Chalking. As exterior paints weather, a dusty film develops on the surface. This dust is called chalk. (Illus. 118) Chalk is actually the residue of the pigments in the top surface of the paint that are left behind as the binders in the paint weather away. To a certain extent, chalking can be desirable. It makes the paint self-cleaning. Stains and dirt that have accumulated on the surface of the paint will

Illus. 116. Mildew.

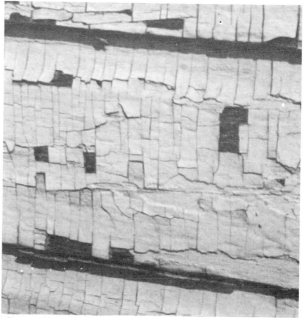

Illus. 117. Alligatoring.

Illus. 118. Chalking.

wash away with the chalk during rainstorms or when the surface is hosed down. When chalking becomes extreme, it becomes a problem. Excessive chalking will create streaks and stains on foundations and sidewalks or on areas of contrasting color. For this reason, contrasting trim should always be painted with a chalk-resistant (not "self-cleaning") paint.

Chalking makes repainting difficult because the loose chalk creates a barrier between the new paint and the old surface. When using latex paint over a chalked surface, you must completely remove all of the chalk by hosing the surface down with water and detergent and scrubbing with a stiff brush. Some oil-based primers and paints will soak through a chalked surface to bond to the firm paint below. If you use this type of

primer first, you can apply latex paint over it.

EXTERIOR PROTECTIVE STAINS

Exterior protective stains differ from the stains discussed earlier in that they form a protective coating on the wood as well as adding color. No additional top coat is needed when these types of stains are applied. They are primarily intended for building exteriors and fences, but they can also be used for outdoor furniture and interior woodwork.

There are two main categories of exterior protective stains: semitransparent and opaque. Semitransparent is the most durable of the two and is preferred when the stain will be applied to new wood. It also has the advantage of letting the grain of the wood show. Opaque stains are also called solid color stains. They totally cover the grain of the wood. They are most often used to restain wood to a color that is substantially different from the old stain. Opaque stains should only be used on vertical surfaces such as walls. Decks and other horizontal surfaces should only be stained with semitransparent stains, because standing water won't affect semitransparent stains as much as it will opaque stains.

Both types of stain are available in oil-based and water-based formulas. The oil-based formula usually contains a large percentage of linseed oil to soak into the wood and preserve it. The water-based stains may include an acrylic resin, or they may use linseed oil that has been emulsified in water.

To provide the most protection, these stains must be worked into the wood by brushing back and forth. If spray equipment or rollers are used to apply the stain, brush over the surface while the stain is still wet to work it into the wood.

5 · Mixing Stains

Although there are literally hundreds of different colors of stains available commercially, there comes a time when none of them exactly fits your needs. You may visualize a particular project with a unique original color, or you may be trying to match a new piece to an existing set of furniture. In any case, you will have to mix your own stain to achieve your goal. Sometimes it's possible to mix two or more commercial stains to achieve the desired result, but you'll usually have more creative control if you mix tinting colors to get the color you want.

In order to mix stains intelligently, you need to know a little about color theory. Colors are classified according to three main criteria; hue, value, and chroma. Hue is what most people call color—red or blue for example. Red, blue, and yellow are the primary colors of pigments; this means that all of the other colors can be made by mixing these colors in different proportions. For example, yellow and blue mixed in equal proportions make green. Yellow and red make orange, and red and blue make violet. Value is determined by the lightness or darkness of a color. Value is altered by the addition of white or black. Adding white to a color lightens its value; the result is called a tint of the original color. When black is added to a color, the result is called a shade; it has a darker value

than the original color. Chroma is the intensity of the color. High intensity colors are brilliant, while low intensity colors are grayish. Every color has a complementary color that will decrease the chroma of a color when the two are mixed. Complementary colors are opposite each other on the color wheel. (Illus. 119)

Mixing colors for stains is slightly different than mixing pure colors such as red and

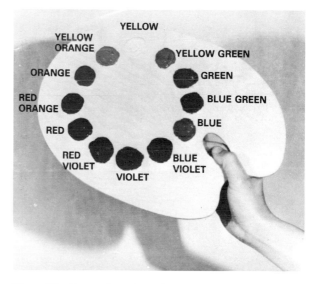

Illus. 119. You mix colors for stains using the same color theory artists use. The color wheel consists of twelve colors. The three primary colors, red, yellow and blue, and the colors that result when they are mixed. Complementary colors are exactly opposite each other on the wheel.

blue. The colors most often used for stains are earth colors that are derived from natural minerals; they are not pure colors, they are mixtures, tints and shades of pure colors. But since they are naturally produced colors, they look better on wood where you are trying to achieve a natural look. Colors used for wood stains usually have a low chroma and a fairly dark value. Colors with a high chroma tend to look very artificial on wood and should be avoided unless you are intentionally trying for an unusual look.

Tinting Colors. Tinting colors are pigments suspended in a liquid vehicle. They are classified by the type of vehicle used. There are three types of tinting colors: oil, Japan, and universal. Oil colors can be used to tint any oil-based product; Japan colors will mix with oil-based and lacquer-based products. Universal tinting colors will tint oil and water-based products. Of the three types, the universal tinting colors are the easiest to use to mix stains. They are more liquid while the other two are a paste. The paste type is harder to mix completely.

Tinting colors are available in a wide range of standard colors that use standard names regardless of the type of vehicle or the manufacturer.

You don't need to buy a whole set of tinting colors to mix your own stains; in fact 90 percent of the time you will only need four colors: burnt umber, yellow ochre, burnt sienna, and zinc white.

Burnt umber is a dark brown color. If you could only have one tinting color, it should be burnt umber. Almost all of the popular shades of brown stain can be made with varying amounts of burnt umber. When you buy your tinting colors, it's a good idea to buy a larger container of burnt umber because it will be a major constituent in almost all stains. Straight burnt umber is the color most commonly thought of as walnut stain.

Yellow ochre is a tannish yellow. Straight yellow ochre is the color of light pine stain. It is used to make light-colored stains or to add a yellow cast to darker stains.

Burnt sienna is reddish brown. It is used for mahogany-colored stains, or when mixed with yellow ochre produces a pleasing orange color used on pine and maple.

Zinc white is used to lighten the above colors.

Pigmented Oil Stain. You can make your own pigmented oil stain very easily. The formula is:

one pint paint thinner
7 oz. boiled linseed oil
½ oz. Japan drier
tinting colors as desired

Turpentine can be substituted for the paint thinner. Japan drier is a product that helps the linseed oil dry. You can substitute an oil-based varnish if you can't find Japan drier. Any of the three types of tinting colors can be used, since they are all compatible with oil. The above formula will make about one quart of stain. The exact amount of stain produced will vary depending on how much tinting color is used.

To mix the stain, first pour about one cup of paint thinner into a container; add the desired tinting colors to the thinner and thoroughly mix. Now add the rest of the ingredients and mix completely. (Illus. 120) If the stain will be stored in the container for a long time it needs an air-tight lid.

The stain is applied exactly the same as commercial pigmented oil stain. (See Chapter 3 for details.)

Varnish Stain. Universal tinting colors, oil colors, and Japan colors are all compatible with oil-based varnish, so you can use them to color varnish to any shade that you wish to create. Mix the tinting colors with a small amount of turpentine first, then add the mixture to the varnish.

Illus. 120. You can make your own pigmented oil stain by mixing paint thinner, boiled linseed oil, Japan drier, and tinting colors.

Lacquer Shading Stain. Lacquer can be tinted with Japan colors to produce a shading stain. Mix the colors in lacquer thinner before adding them to the lacquer. Chapter 3 describes the uses for shading stains.

Water Stains. The aniline dyes used to make water stains are not available as tinting colors; so to custom mix true aniline water stains, you have to intermix commercially prepared stains. Mix the powdered stains with water before combining colors. Universal tinting colors are water compatible, so you can slightly alter the color of a water stain by adding a little universal tinting color. But remember that tinting colors are pigments while water stains are dyes, so by adding a pigment you are losing some of the clarity of the water stain.

You can make a water stain that is very similar in appearance to aniline dye stains from transparent artist's watercolors. The colors come in tubes and are available from art supply dealers. Many of the colors use the same standard names as tinting colors,

so you can easily choose the ones you want. Mix the colors together as they come from the tube, then thin them with water. Apply the stain the same way you would apply aniline dye stain.

COLOR MIXING FORMULAS

The following formulas are meant to give you a general starting place in your search for your own individual color choice. By varying the proportions of the colors, you can considerably alter the resulting stain. Color intensity is best altered by increasing or decreasing the amount of the colors listed. Adding white or black to the formula not only lightens or darkens the intensity; it changes the whole character of the stain. White tends to give the stain a limed effect if used too extensively. Black is probably the most widely misused tinting color. Black is commonly added to stains under the misconception that it will darken the color. What actually happens is that the black pigment overpowers the other pigments and totally changes the look of the stain. Black pigments have a tendency to collect mainly in the pores or soft areas of the wood, greatly accentuating the grain. You will notice that none of the formulas listed contain black unless they are specifically a black or grey stain like ebony, silver-grey, or mission oak. Burnt umber is much better than lamp black for darkening a stain. You can add burnt umber to any of the brown stains to darken them without greatly changing their basic character.

The formulas include amounts that indicate how much of each pigment should be used to make one quart of pigmented oil stain. The same proportions apply to other types of stains.

The first group of formulas use only the four basic tinting colors discussed earlier. The second group of stains include other colors in addition to the basic four.

Stains Using The Four Basic Tinting Colors

Walnut
6 oz. burnt umber

Red Mahogany
6 oz. burnt sienna

Brown Mahogany
6 oz. burnt umber
2 oz. burnt sienna

Dark Oak
6 oz. burnt umber
1 oz. burnt sienna
½ oz. yellow ochre

Light Oak
1 oz. burnt umber
1 oz. yellow ochre

Cherry
4 oz. burnt sienna
1 oz. burnt umber
¼ oz. yellow ochre

Natural Pine
4 oz. yellow ochre
2 oz. zinc white
1 oz. burnt umber

Pickled Pine
4 oz. zinc white
1 oz. yellow ochre
¼ oz. burnt umber

Antique Pine
3 oz. burnt umber
2 oz. yellow ochre
1 oz. zinc white
¼ oz. burnt sienna

Limed Oak
6 oz. zinc white
1 oz. yellow ochre
¼ oz. burnt umber

Honey Maple
6 oz. yellow ochre
1 oz. burnt sienna
¼ oz. burnt umber

Stains Using Additional Colors

Medium Dark Walnut
5 oz. vandyke brown
4 oz. burnt umber

Dark Walnut
7 oz. vandyke brown

Bright Red Mahogany
5 oz. burnt sienna
1 oz. raw umber
½ oz. vermilion red

Dark Brown Mahogany
6 oz. vandyke brown
1 oz. raw umber
1 oz. rose pink

Pumpkin Maple
5 oz. burnt sienna
a touch of ultramarine blue

Yellow Maple
3 oz. raw sienna
1 oz. raw umber

Honey Pine
4 oz. yellow ochre
1 oz. raw sienna

Light Cherry
3 oz. raw sienna
3 oz. burnt sienna
¼ oz. rose pink

Mission Oak
3 oz. vandyke brown
1 oz. burnt umber
2 oz. lamp black

Ebony
8 oz. ivory black
¼ oz. rose pink
⅛ oz. Prussian blue

Weathered Silver Grey
2 oz. lamp black
3 oz. zinc white
¼ oz. raw sienna

6 · Finishing Problem Woods

Most wood will accept almost any type of finish with good results, but there are a few problem woods that are difficult to finish with standard methods. They are pine, fir, wood with sap streaks and uneven coloring, oily wood, and rough cut wood.

Pine and Fir

Pine and fir are woods that are commonly used by do-it-yourselfers for projects, and yet these are two of the most difficult woods to stain well. (Illus. 121) Pine in its natural state with only a clear finish is a beautiful wood with a very clear, subtle grain; but usually when it is stained, it becomes cloudy or muddy looking and the grain stands out much too prominently. (Illus. 122) Other soft woods such as hemlock, spruce, and cypress aren't as widely used, but they pose the same problems as pine for the wood finisher. Some light-colored hardwoods, birch in particular, will sometimes look muddy when a very dark stain is applied. If you have a problem with this, try one of the remedies used for pine. Fir plywood is an even bigger problem, because the wood has been rotary cut from the log, resulting in a very wild, unnatural looking grain that stands out prominently when a stain is applied. (Illus. 123)

Light-colored stains are not as big a prob-

Illus. 121. Pine is one of the most commonly used woods for unfinished furniture. When it is finished properly, a beautiful piece is the result. However, if the wrong finishing procedures are used, the resulting finish may be disappointing.

lem as dark stains on these woods. Dark stains will stain the soft parts of the grain but leave the harder parts practically the natural color. But even light-colored stains tend to have a muddy look.

There are several remedies to these problems. Water stains work better on fir and pine than oil stains do. Latex stain also seems

Illus. 122. This is an example of the muddy look that stained pine sometimes exhibits.

Illus. 123. Fir that is rotary cut exhibits a wild grain pattern.

to have an advantage, if it is wiped off almost as soon as it is applied. If you want to use an oil stain, try applying a coat of a tung oil or Danish oil finish first and apply the stain over that. This will partially seal the grain and help the stain to be absorbed more uniformly.

One type of oil stain comes as a paste or gel; this type doesn't soak into the wood very much, and so you can even out the color by wiping to a greater degree than you can with stains that penetrate deeper.

Another way to get the stain to be absorbed more uniformly is to seal the wood with a coat of shellac that has been thinned with alcohol to a one-pound cut. If you want a dark finish, try using orange shellac as the sealer; for a very dark finish, apply button shellac. This method will help the stain to coat the wood more uniformly. After the shellac is dry, sand it lightly with 320 grit sandpaper then wipe on a pigmented oil stain. The shellac will prevent the stain from soaking into the wood very much. Since the stain must adhere to the surface of the shellac to color the wood, it may be necessary to

leave it on the wood for a longer time than normal before wiping. Wipe the stain in long straight strokes, not in a circular motion. The wiping is especially important on fir plywood, because you can help to hide some of the wild grain. Use a coarse cloth like burlap (hessian) and wipe lightly in long straight strokes with the grain direction. The burlap will leave small lines in the stain that will tend to visually straighten out the wild grain patterns of the wood.

Using orange shellac or button shellac as the top coat will even out the color further.

Shading stains work well on these woods. One of the best ways to get a really uniform dark color on pine or fir is to stain it first with a water stain and when that coat is dry apply a coat of shading stain over it. Shading stains are useful for light colors as well; you can get a beautifully glowing light pine effect by sealing the bare wood with lacquer sanding sealer and then applying a light-color lacquer shading stain. Light will be reflected off the almost white color of the sealed wood. This will give the finish a very nice inner glow. (Illus. 124, 125)

Illus. 124. These pine samples were stained using the techniques described. Left to right, the first sample was given a coat of orange shellac, over which a pigmented wiping stain was used. The second sample was first given a coat of clear penetrating oil, after which a penetrating oil stain was applied. The third sample was initially stained with a water stain. Shading stain was applied over the water stain.

Sap Streaks and Color Variation

Other problem woods are those that contain sap streaks or wide variations in color. (Illus. 126) If the affected area is darker than the desired finish, you can selectively bleach the area first. If the area is too light, try applying a second coat of stain to that area only. If the color variation is not too great, you can even out the color by using a wiping stain and wiping the area more or less than the surrounding wood. (Illus. 127) When there is a difference in hue between two boards in the same project, you can bring them closer in color by adding some tinting color to the stain. Try to determine what the difference in color is, so you will know how to neutralize the difference. For example, mahogany can vary from a yellowish brown to a reddish brown. If you glued up a table top from two pieces of mahogany and one had a yellow cast while the other was more of a red color, you could even the two out by adding a little yellow ochre to the stain for the red side and

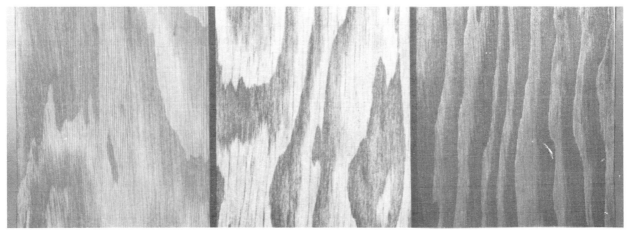

Illus. 125. These fir samples were stained using the techniques described. The sample on the left was given a coat of orange shellac over which a pigmented wiping stain was used. The middle sample was first given a coat of clear penetrating oil, after which a penetrating oil stain was applied. The sample on the right was initially stained with a water stain. Shading stain was applied over the water stain.

111

Illus. 126. This piece of walnut contains dark heartwood and light sapwood. Ordinary staining techniques will not even out this wide a color variation.

Illus. 127. This is the same piece of walnut after being stained using the techniques described in the text.

adding some burnt sienna to the yellow side. The result will be a uniform brown. You can see why this works by referring to the color wheel in Chapter 5. Red and yellow make orange; brown is a dark shade of orange. By combining the yellow ochre with the reddish color of the one side, the resulting color is brown. The burnt sienna is a reddish color, so it combines with the yellowish board to also make brown. You can use this technique with any combination of color variations; all it takes is some familiarity with the color wheel and an ability to judge what the actual color difference is. If two boards are about the same hue, but one is too intense of a color, you can try adding a little tinting color that is the complement of the color you want to tone down. Complementary colors are opposite each other on the color wheel.

Another problem encountered is that end grain will stain darker than the rest of the board. This can be corrected by applying a coat of tung oil or Danish oil finish to the end grain first or seal the ends with a coat of thinned shellac.

Some pieces of wood, especially quartersawed varieties, will exhibit a quality called grain reflection. The amount of light that the grain reflects varies with the viewing angle and the angle that the light strikes the wood. This can make the wood appear lighter from one viewing angle and darker from another. Usually no attempt to compensate for this difference should be made because any attempt to hide the difference will simply make it more obvious from another angle. Normally, grain reflection is regarded as a beautifying aspect of wood that emphasizes its natural character since it cannot be duplicated in manmade products, so simply enjoy this characteristic without trying to alter it. When the wood will remain in a fixed position and will be viewed under constant light conditions you may consider attempting to even out the differences. For example, a panelled wall that contains pieces with both vertical and horizontal grain may show all of the horizontal grain darker than the vertical grain. In that case you may want to apply additional stain to the horizontal pieces to give the wall a more uniform look.

Oily Woods

Some of the more exotic woods such as teak, rosewood, cocobola, and lignum vitae contain natural oils that interfere with the finishing process. (Illus. 128) Sometimes varnish applied to these woods will refuse to dry and will remain tacky indefinitely. Lacquer may not adhere well to these woods.

The best solution to the problem of finishing oily woods is to use an oil finish. Penetrating oil finishes will combine with and harden the natural oils present in the wood. Some companies make a special oil finish specifically for these woods. If you don't want to use a penetrating oil finish, you will have to remove as much of the oil as you can from the wood before applying a finish. To do this, flood the wood with alcohol or lacquer thinner and brush into the grain with a stiff scrub brush. Change the solvent frequently. After washing with solvent, let the wood dry and then apply a sealer coat of shellac or lacquer sanding sealer. From this point you can finish the wood as usual. Another alternative is to first apply a penetrating oil finish as a sealer; let this coat cure for several days to a week, then apply varnish over the oil finish.

Rough Wood

Rough-cut lumber has recently become a popular material for room panelling and rustic cabinet work. The rough texture can present a problem if you want to maintain the rough look and yet protect and color the wood.

Rough cedar is a popular material for interior room panelling. If cedar is left unfinished, it will darken with age. This may be desirable in some cases; but if you want to

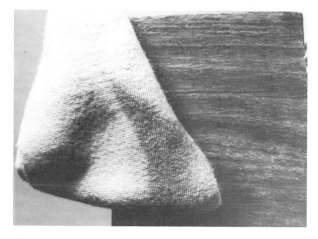

Illus. 128. This piece of freshly planed rosewood has so much oil on the surface that it leaves a stain on a rag wiped over the board.

keep the look of fresh cut cedar without adding any color to the wood, you can spray a light coat of lacquer sanding sealer on the wood. Hold the spray gun farther from the work than is normal and set the gun to deliver a light dry spray. If the spray is too wet, it will soak into the wood and darken it. The idea is to get the sealer to dry almost as soon as it touches the surface.

In areas where rough wood will be touched frequently, it is desirable to apply a finish that will glue down the loose slivers to prevent them from getting into your skin. Latex varnish is one of the best materials to use for this. Because it is water based, it will tend to raise the grain and accentuate the rough-cut look; and yet its thick glue-like consistency will firmly attach all of the loose wood fibres to prevent slivers. (Illus. 129) When you want to alter the color of the wood, you can use either a latex stain or one of the exterior linseed oil stains especially formulated for rough wood.

Old barn lumber is especially prized for its acquired patina. In most cases it should be left unfinished to avoid destroying the natural weathered look. If a finish must be applied, spray lacquer sanding sealer in the manner described above. One problem with

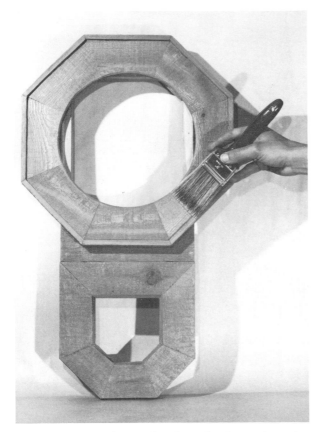

Illus. 129. Rough-cut lumber is becoming increasingly popular for rustic room accessories such as this clock. Brushing on a latex varnish accentuates the rough look while gluing down loose slivers.

barn lumber is that any newly cut edges will not match the weathered surface. The best way to handle this problem is to design the work in a way that won't show any fresh-cut wood; use mitre joints whenever possible. When it is impossible to hide the fresh-cut wood, stain it with a custom mixed stain that is as close as possible to the general color of the weathered surface.

Here is a recipe for a stain that will match most weathered wood: Pour about half a cup of paint thinner into a small container. Add enough zinc white and lamp black to make a silver grey color that is close to the general color of weathered wood. Add about two tablespoons of boiled linseed oil and one tablespoon of flat varnish to the stain. Now use some very thick oil colors. Add small chunks of burnt sienna, raw umber, and burnt umber to the mixture. Don't try to mix these thoroughly into the stain. The purpose of these colors is to create random variations in the color as the stain is wiped onto the wood.

Apply the stain with a rag to the cut edges of the barn wood. As a particle of the unmixed pigments reaches the surface, the rag will smear it into a long streak simulating the variations found in the original surface. This technique requires some experimentation to find the correct color mix to exactly match a particular piece; but where the cut edges are not too conspicuous, it is only necessary to give the wood a general weathered look to sufficiently disguise it.

7 · Hand-Rubbed Finishes

It's hard to find a finish that compares to the classic beauty of a hand-rubbed finish. It possesses a silky smooth texture and a fine sheen that can range anywhere from matte to high gloss. The traditional method of producing a hand-rubbed finish involves the use of two very fine abrasives, pumice and rottenstone, to smooth and polish the surface of the hardened top coat of finishing material. Rubbed finishes are most commonly used on flat surfaces like table tops because it is difficult to rub parts with recesses, carvings or intricate curves.

Not all finishes can be rubbed. If you intend to rub out a varnish coat, use a varnish formulated for rubbing. Rubbing varnishes are in the short oil category. Synthetic varnishes like polyurethane can be rubbed out; some are specially formulated for the purpose. Lacquer is well suited to rubbing. Shellac can be rubbed out if water is not used as a lubricant.

To produce a traditional rubbed finish make sure that the top coat has had plenty of time to harden, then sand it smooth with wet-or-dry sandpaper. If the top coat is very smooth, you can use 600 grit paper; normally it's best to start with 400 grit paper to smooth out any dust nibs or surface irregularities, then switch to 600 grit for a final sanding. Lubricate the sandpaper by sponging water on the wood surface or by pouring on a little paraffin oil. Paraffin oil is a mineral oil formulated for use in rubbing; it is also called rubbing oil. After sanding, the surface should have a uniform dull matte look.

For the next step, you will need a solid block of hard felt. Wood finishing supply dealers sell them specifically for rubbing. (Illus. 130) You will also need some pumice; it is available in several grades. "FFF" is the finest and most commonly used. Lubricate the surface to be rubbed with either paraffin oil or water. Paraffin oil is the traditional lubricant, but it has the disadvantage of being hard to remove after the rubbing is complete.

Illus. 130. A hard felt block made specifically for rubbing is the best tool to use for a hand-rubbed finish.

115

However, a rag dampened with paint thinner will usually remove any stubborn spots of oil. Paraffin oil also may react with some finishes causing them to turn milky white; however, this is rare if you use a finish that is recommended by the manufacturer for rubbing. Water makes the pumice cut faster than it does with oil, and it leaves no residue on the finish; but it can't be used to rub shellac and it may make the pumice cut so fast that it is hard to control. If you add a little soap to the water, it will behave more like oil and be easier to control; the soap will also retard evaporation so you won't have to add water to the surface as often.

Now sprinkle a little pumice onto the surface and use the felt block to rub it back and forth with the grain. Pumice becomes finer as it wears during the rubbing process. Because of this, it is best to sprinkle enough pumice onto the surface to do the entire job at once. As the pumice wears down, the finish it produces becomes progressively smoother; if you add fresh pumice in a particular spot, the finish in that area will be duller than the rest of the surface because the new pumice is coarser than the used pumice. If you need to add more pumice, be sure to rub it uniformly over the entire surface. Occasionally wipe away the film of pumice and lubricant to check on your progress. When all of the marks left by the sandpaper are gone, you are done. If you want a satin finish, simply clean off all of the residue left from the pumice and lubricant and apply a good quality paste wax to the finish. If you want a higher gloss, an additional step is necessary.

To achieve a high gloss by rubbing, switch to rottenstone. Use a different felt pad so that no trace of pumice will be left in the pad. Thoroughly clean all of the pumice from the wood surface. Then lubricate and rub the surface with rottenstone the same as you did with the pumice. Periodically wipe away the residue to see how the shine is progressing; when you've reached the shine you're after,

wipe away all of the residue and apply paste wax.

This traditional method of hand rubbing has produced fine results for hundreds of years, but it is very time consuming and laborious, so modern technology has developed several ways to achieve a rubbed effect with less work. A power rubbing machine takes a lot of the work out of rubbing out a finish. The procedure used is the same as for hand rubbing, but the machine does most of the work. (Illus. 131)

Another modern development is the introduction of premixed rubbing compound that contains its own lubricant. These compounds were initially developed to rub out automotive lacquer, but they are equally good for rubbing out wood finishes. Some wood finishing companies now make compounds specifically for wood, but if you can't find this type the automotive type is readily available at auto supply stores. (Illus. 132) The compound comes in two grades: rubbing compound which is white in color and corresponds to pumice, and polishing compound which is red and performs like rottenstone. These compounds are used just like pumice and rottenstone, except that no additional lubricant is needed. The com-

Illus. 131. An air-operated rubbing machine takes much of the work out of the rubbing process.

116

Illus. 132. Pumice and rottenstone are both dry powders. Polishing compound is a paste that contains its own lubricant.

pound comes in a paste form. If it begins to dry out as rubbing progresses, a few drops of water will restore it to the proper consistency. The compound can be easily removed with a damp rag, leaving no oily residue.

Another new development is 1200 grit wet-or-dry sandpaper which is available from mail-order woodworking supply companies. You can achieve almost the same effect as a pumice rubbed finish by simply wet sanding the finish with this ultrafine sandpaper.

Steel wool is often used to produce a satin rubbed effect. Use 4/0 steel wool. Lubricate the surface with paste furniture wax or a wax made specifically for steel wool rubbing. Rub the steel wool with the grain direction. The wax prevents the steel wool from leaving deep scratches.

8 · Wood Graining

Wood graining is the art of duplicating the grain of an expensive wood on the surface of a less expensive substitute. The process is hundreds of years old. It experienced a major renaissance in the mid-1800's when the American pioneers went west. They found that the hardwoods they had become used to on the east coast were scarce in the west, so they used wood graining to make the native red pine look like walnut, oak, maple, or cherry. After the railroads made transportation of lumber practical from one area of the country to another, wood graining began to die out. But recently there has been a renewed interest in wood graining as a method of holding down the cost of do-it-yourself projects. In almost every project there are some parts that can be made of a cheaper material if it matches the wood used elsewhere. The shelves and back of a bookcase are an example. By using fir plywood, hardboard, or particle board for these parts, the cost of a project can be kept down. Wood graining will make it match the wood in the rest of the case.

A lot of inexpensive unfinished furniture is made of particleboard. (Illus. 133) Wood graining is a practical way to finish this type of furniture. You can achieve the look of real wood at a fraction of the cost of hardwood by graining particleboard. (Illus. 134)

Illus. 133. This inexpensive particle board nightstand is a good candidate for wood graining.

Illus. 134. After wood graining is complete, it's hard to believe this is the same nightstand shown above.

Wood-graining techniques are also used to alter the grain of some woods like birch or lauan (Philippine mahogany) when these woods are used in a project along with other more prominently grained woods like oak or ash.

The first step in graining is to apply a ground coat of flat latex or oil-base paint. Use a paint that is the same color as the lightest part of the wood you are trying to imitate; you can use tinting colors mixed in white paint to achieve any ground color you want. Solid color acrylic stains that are normally used for the exterior of houses make a good ground coat; they are available in a wide range of wood tones. The direction of the wood graining is not dependent on the direction of the actual grain of the underlying wood, and manmade substances like particle board don't have any grain direction, so before applying the ground coat, decide on the grain direction for each part and then apply the ground coat with all brush strokes in the direction of the grain. Usually the grain direction should follow the longest dimension of the piece.

A ground coat is not always necessary on hardboard or particle board parts that won't receive close scrutiny. In fact, the small flecks of wood visible on the surface may enhance the appearance of the finished grain. Another instance where no ground coat is used is when you want to add a more interesting grain pattern to an otherwise uninteresting piece of hardwood. The lower grades of lauan are an example. Some pieces of lauan have practically no visible grain patterns; their only characteristic is a uniform pattern of pores distributed evenly over the entire surface. You can add interest to a board like this by using one of the graining techniques described later.

After the ground coat is dry, the graining stain is applied. The most important consideration is the consistency of the stain. It must be heavy-bodied and fairly fast-drying or the grain pattern will flow together. Traditional wood grainers mixed their own graining stains, adding a thickening agent called megilp to make it the correct consistency; today there are several products that can be used as a graining stain, so it usually is not necessary to prepare your own stain. Antiquing ink, varnish stain, or heavy-bodied stain work well. You can use a latex stain over a latex ground coat, but don't use it on bare particle board because it makes the particles swell, giving a bumpy surface.

The graining stain can be worked with special tools or applied freehand to achieve a number of different effects.

GRAINING TOOLS

The old-time wood grainers used many tools to produce realistic grains. Until recently, they were not widely available commercially. Now a few companies are starting to market some types of graining tools; but anyone serious about graining will still have to make most of his own tools, at least until a complete line of wood-graining tools is reintroduced to the market.

One of the most useful wood-graining tools is called a *block cushion grainer*; it consists of a piece of rubber moulded with semicircular ridges. The rubber face is attached to a block of wood that holds the rubber in a curved shape. A handle attaches to the block. This one tool is capable of producing almost an infinite variety of realistic looking grain patterns. This is one tool that is again on the market, but the selection is still very limited. Most commercial models are only about four inches wide, which limits their use to small work. You can make your own grainers in any size you choose. Also, by varying the size and spacing of the grooves, you can alter the effects that it will produce. (Illus. 135)

To make your own grainers, you first need to make a mould for the rubber face. Cut a circle of ¾-in. hardwood. The circle can be

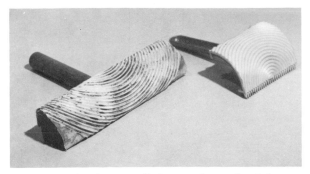

Illus. 135. The large graining tool on the left was made using the procedure described in the text. The smaller tool on the right is a commercial model.

any size that will fit on your lathe. It's best to make a large mould because you can use it for smaller tools if you wish. Mount the circle on a lathe faceplate and using a small skew chisel, cut V-shaped grooves ⅛ in. deep and ⅛ in. apart, until the entire face is covered with concentric circles. (Illus. 136)

An easy way to get the spacing for the grooves of your first mould is to touch the teeth of an eight-point saw to the face of the mould with the lathe running. Each tooth will make a scratch indicating the center of the groove. This will give you an average spacing that produces a grainer useful for most work. Later you can experiment with more or less spacing; closely spaced grooves make a grain that looks more like hardwood, while widely spaced grooves produce a grain that looks closer to pine.

It is important that all of the grooves be of equal depth; it is the bottom of the groove in the mould that produces the top point of the ridge on the grainer. All of these ridges must be equal in height so they will all contact the work uniformly.

If you don't have a lathe, you can use an ordinary electric drill. Mount it in a drill stand. Attach the stand to a piece of plywood and nail a short piece of 2 × 4 to the front. The 2 × 4 serves as a tool rest.

A drill won't handle a mould much larger than six inches in diameter, so if you want a really large grainer you will need a lathe.

Illus. 136. The mould is made on a lathe. Cut V-shaped grooves with a skew chisel to cover the mould with concentric circles. Make all of the grooves the same depth to avoid high spots in the finished grainer that would make the tool difficult to use.

Drill a ¼-in. hole in the exact center of the wood disc. Slip a ¼-in. bolt 1½ in. long through the hole and secure with a nut and washer on the back. Now put the bolt in the drill chuck and adjust so the face of the mould is ¹⁄₁₆ in. from the 2 × 4. (Illus. 137)

After all the cuts are made, remove the mould from the faceplate and give the turn-

Illus. 137. An electric drill mounted in a drill stand can be used to make the mould if you don't have a lathe. A piece of 2×4 serves as a tool rest.

ing a good coat of penetrating sealer and then wax with paste wax.

The grainer is made from silicone rubber caulking. You will need a lot of it, so buy a caulking gun cartridge of it rather than buying it in tubes. Cover the mould with a layer of silicone rubber caulking about ⅛ inch thick. (The full mould makes two tools; so if you want only one, cover half the mould.) Put a rag on top of the rubber and smooth it out. Rub over the rag to force the caulking into all of the grooves in the mould. Leave the rag on top of the caulking to form a reinforced backing. Let the caulking cure for at least 24 hours. (Illus. 138)

When it has cured, peel the rubber from the mould. (Illus. 139) Make a backing from a piece of wood about two inches square and as long as the diameter of the mould. Use a plane or a sander to round off one corner of the block so that it resembles a piece of quarter-round moulding. Drill a half-inch hole in the center of each of the two remaining flat faces for a handle. Cut the rubber to fit the backing and glue it to the curved surface with contact cement. Fold it over the corners and staple for added strength. Cut a six-inch length of dowel for a handle.

To use the tool, apply a heavy coat of graining stain to the work with a brush. (Illus. 140)

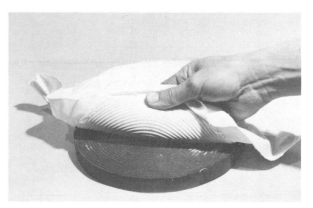

Illus. 139. After the silicone rubber has cured, it can be easily peeled from the mould.

Push the graining tool across the surface, lifting the handle to rock the face of the tool. (Illus. 141) Wide boards require several passes with the grainer to cover the surface with a grain pattern. Overlap each pass slightly so there won't be any ungrained areas left between the passes. The larger homemade grainers will cover a wide board in one or two passes, while the smaller commercial models will require many passes to cover the same board. The effect produced when many passes are made with a small grainer looks like several narrow boards were glued together to make one wide board;

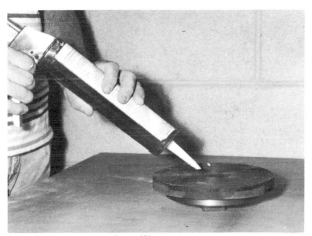

Illus. 138. Apply the silicone rubber to the mould with a caulking gun.

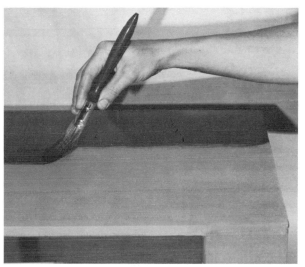

Illus. 140. After the ground coat is dry, brush on a coat of graining stain.

Illus. 141. While the graining stain is still wet, push the graining tool over the surface.

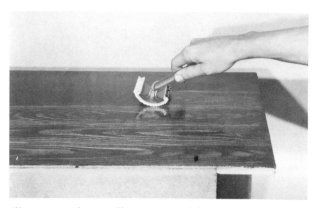

Illus. 142. The smaller commercial graining tool must be passed over wide boards many times to completely cover the surface with grain.

the effect is not unnatural looking and may be sufficient for many types of work. (Illus. 142)

Combinations of forward and rocking motions produce a variety of results. Illustration 143 shows some combinations. Examples (A) and (B) were made by rapidly rocking the grainer while pushing across the board. To reproduce (C) and (D), gradually and continuously raise the handle as you push the grainer across the board. The knot in (E) was made by rapidly raising and lowering the handle. Use a straight through motion on the rest of the stroke. Gradually raising and then

lowering the handle will produce a grain like (F). No rocking motion at all is used to make (G). Slowly raise the handle while pushing across to reproduce (H).

The purpose of having two handle positions is also illustrated in examples (A) through (D).

(A) and (B) were both made with the same motion. The only difference was the position of the handle. The same is true for (C) and (D). For (A) and (C) the handle was in the position closest to the large diameter half circles in the rubber. (B) and (D) were made

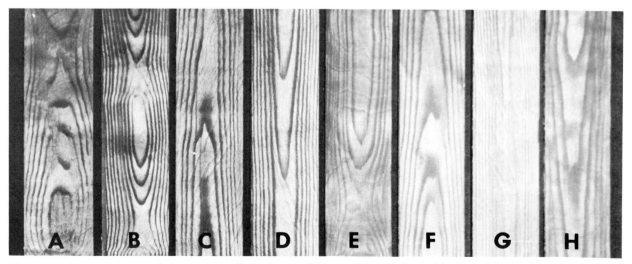

Illus. 143. Here are some of the many grains it is possible to produce using a block cushion grainer and how the natural grain of a board can be disguised with this tool. All of the grains were produced on pieces cut from the same board. No ground coat was used.

Illus. 144. Brushing over the completed grain makes it look more realistic by fanning out the lines and breaking up areas of solid color.

Illus. 145. Here a commercial comb is being used to simulate straight-grained mahogany. One side of the comb has irregularly spaced wide teeth that were used to make the prominent grain pattern. The side in use in the picture has fine, evenly spaced teeth. They are being used to break up the larger lines.

with the handle next to the small diameter half circles.

If you aren't satisfied with the first results, simply pass the grainer over the same section again; you can make several passes over the same area before it is necessary to apply more stain. If the grain runs together after a while, the stain is too liquid; let it dry for a few minutes and try again.

You can make the graining look even more realistic by brushing over it with a dry brush. Brush in the grain direction to feather out the grain lines. (Illus. 144)

Graining combs. Graining combs are another means of producing a grain on wood. Specially made graining combs are best but they are hard to come by; you can experiment with ordinary hair combs or thin pieces of wood, rubber or plastic with teeth cut into them. The main requirement is that the teeth must all be the same height so that they will all touch the wood surface at the same time. A sawtooth glue spreader (the type used to apply linoleum paste) can also be used as a graining comb. Coarse-weave cloth such as burlap (hessian) or cheesecloth can be used in a manner similar to a comb; fold the cloth into a pad and use one edge just like the teeth of a comb. A piece of cardboard inside

of the pad will add some stiffness if you need it.

Use a brush to apply a thin coat of stain over the ground coat. Drag the teeth of the comb over the stain. The teeth will scrape the stain off of the areas they touch, making a lighter line. (Illus. 145) The grain produced by a comb is similar to the straight grain of quarter-sawed wood. You can heighten the quarter-sawed effect by dragging the comb lightly over the work a second time. On the second pass, move the comb at a slight angle to the first pass so that the two sets of lines cross each other at a very shallow angle. This technique reproduces the pore pattern of quarter-sawed oak. There is a tendency among beginning wood grainers to wave the comb back and forth, making a very wiggily grain; but if you look at a piece of quarter-sawed wood, you will see that the grain lines are really fairly straight.

Ray marker. If you look closely at a piece of plain-sawed oak, you will see that the entire surface is covered with hundreds of tiny dashes. These dashes are the ends of the medullary rays. A ray marker is a tool that will reproduce these dashes. The ray marker

123

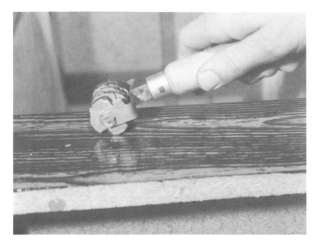

Illus. 146. A ray marker produces small dash marks.

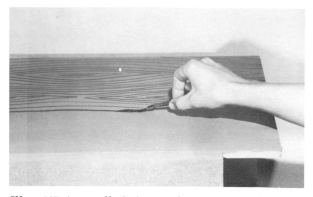

Illus. 147. A camel's-hair sword striper is used to paint in the grain lines in freehand graining. Notice how the brush is held nearly parallel to the surface.

has a set of wheels that rotate independently of each other on a common axle. Each wheel has a series of dashes embossed on its edge.

To use the ray marker, first reproduce a plain-sawed grain on the board; then while the stain is still wet, run the ray marker over the grain in straight parallel lines running with the grain. (Illus. 146) If you want an even more realistic effect, let the stain dry, then dip the ray marker in some stain that is either darker or lighter than the stain used first. Run the marker across the entire surface of the board in straight lines parallel to the grain direction.

FREEHAND GRAINING

So far, all of the graining methods described have relied on some mechanical means of producing the grain; in freehand graining, you paint the grain on just like an artist paints a picture. The biggest requirement for freehand graining is an intimate knowledge of the wood you are trying to reproduce. Before trying your hand at freehand graining, study several samples of the wood you want to copy.

One of the most important tools for freehand graining is a good camel's-hair sword striper. This brush has very long, soft fila-ments. You hold this type of brush at a very low angle to the work and drag it along so that the long filaments trail behind it in a straight line. (Illus. 147) Use the sword striper to draw in all of the grain lines; at first it may help to have a sample of real wood close by to determine how the lines should look.

At this point, the lines will look rather unnatural because of their uniformity; to remedy this, brush over the entire surface of the work with a fan-top graining brush or any regular paint brush. Brush lightly in straight lines with the grain. This brushing out will fan out and break up the grain lines. (Illus. 148) Freehand graining takes a lot of practice and study of wood samples, but it is useful when you want to produce special effects such as book-matched grain patterns, burl patterns, quarter-sawed ray patterns or other patterns that can't be produced with mechanical grainers.

Overgraining

Overgraining blends the grain lines produced either mechanically or freehand into a more uniform-looking grain. Although it can be used with mechanical graining, it is most important in freehand graining, because the grain lines that are painted on in freehand

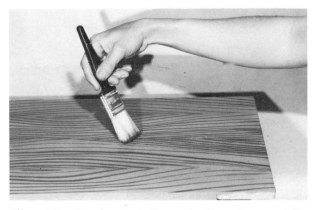

Illus. 148. Fanning out the grain lines is especially important in freehand graining.

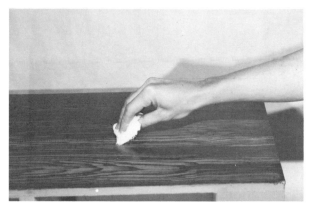

Illus. 149. Overgraining gives the completed grain a more natural look.

graining are so distinct from the ground color.

Let the first grain pattern dry, then seal it with a sealer that is compatible with the materials you are using. Next brush on a thin coat of stain; use graining combs or a pad of coarse cloth to produce a second grain pattern over the first. This graining should be a subtle grain, usually just straight parallel lines. (Illus. 149)

FINISH COAT

After all of the graining coats have dried, you can apply any top coat that is compatible with the stains and ground coat used. Varnish is probably the safest. Lacquer or shellac may dissolve the stain or the ground coat and ruin all of your work.

9 · Chemical Stains

Wood is impregnated with hundreds of chemicals as it grows. The exact chemical composition of a piece of wood depends on the type of soil it grew in, the climate at the time it was growing, and the species of tree. Tannin is one chemical that is found to a greater or lesser degree in almost all wood. The natural color of wood depends on the chemicals present in the wood. These chemicals will react with other chemicals to create new compounds of differing colors. This fact makes the process of chemical staining possible. Through experimentation over the years wood finishers have found certain chemicals that will alter the color of some species of wood.

Quite a few woods can be stained by chemical methods, but the best results are obtained with woods that are high in tannin. Oak, walnut, chestnut, and mahogany are all high-tannin woods.

Chemical stains penetrate deeper into the wood than any other type of stain and they are the most permanent.

Chemical stains are not for the novice; they are often unpredictable and the chemicals are almost always dangerous, but for the advanced finisher chemical stains offer some distinct advantages. First, they provide a clarity of grain that is even superior to water stain. This is because chemical stains don't add any color to the wood; they alter the existing color. Chemical stains have the ability to bring out grain details like birds' eyes or crotch grain that may be obscured by other stains. (Illus. 150) Natural wood has slight variations in color from one part of the grain to another; ordinary stains tend to even out these color variations. If you want to keep that natural look, chemical stains are a better alternative because they won't conceal the color variations, and may enhance them.

Illus. 150. Chemical stains have the ability to bring out grain details like these birds'-eyes. The board on the left was treated with ammonia, while the sample on the right was left untreated.

Many of the chemicals discussed in this chapter will be hard to buy; they don't have any household use, and so they are only available from chemical wholesalers. Sometimes they will only be available in large quantities. These chemicals are listed for the finisher who wants to experiment with them, but be prepared to do some extensive shopping around to find them.

Most chemical stains involve a reaction between tannin in the wood and the stain; since the tannin content of wood is not constant even within one species, the color achieved may vary from board to board. Because of this, you should plan ahead in the early stages of the construction of the project. Whenever possible, all of the boards in a project should be from the same tree; however, this is hard to accomplish unless the project is a small one and can be built from a single board. Before selecting the lumber to be used in the project, test small samples of each board with the chemical stain you plan to use. This way you will be sure that the color produced is what you expected. Use the test samples to group the boards according to color, so you can match all of the boards used in the project. If you must use boards that vary widely in tannin content, you can add tannin to the boards that stain lighter. Professionals use a dilute solution of tannic acid, but strong tea works as well and is safer to use. Apply this with a sponge or brush to the board before applying a chemical stain.

Chemical stains will react with metal hardware to create undesirable dark stains in the wood around the hardware, so don't attach any metal to the project before staining. Even nails can react with the stain, but they usually won't be a problem if they are set below the wood surface.

Putty and wood filler will not be colored by chemical stains, so they should always be applied after staining and then colored to match.

Safety Precautions

Almost all of the chemicals used as stains are either poisonous, caustic, harmful, or irritating in some way, so use them at your own risk and exercise caution when using them. Many chemicals once considered safe as wood stains have recently come under suspicion as being hazardous to your health. Some of the health and safety hazards associated with these chemicals are detailed in the list of chemicals used to make stains; however, new information is constantly being uncovered, so it's a good idea to check with a knowledgeable source before using these chemicals. Don't use poisonous chemicals to finish children's furniture or for items that will come into contact with food. Safety goggles and neoprene gloves are a must when working with chemicals; a rubber lab apron is also advisable when working with acids and other caustic chemicals. A respirator should be worn when using chemicals that produce toxic fumes; an air-supplied respirator is best. Always keep chemicals in their original containers and read and follow all cautions listed on the container. Keep the chemicals out of the reach of children.

Don't use chemical stains on wood that has been bleached with chlorine bleach; poisonous chlorine gas could result.

When working with acids, remember that to dilute an acid always add the acid to the water a little at a time. If water is poured into the acid, a violent reaction may take place that will spray acid out of the container. When you use any chemical stain for the first time, test a small sample of wood with a dilute solution of the stain to check for any unexpected reactions. It is best not to mix any of these chemicals together, because some may react violently when mixed. If you want to use more than one chemical on the wood, apply each one as a separate coat, wash the wood thoroughly and let it dry before applying any other chemicals.

Mixing Chemical Stains

The chemicals used to make stains usually come in three forms: liquid, powdered, and crystals. Before they can be applied as stain, they all need to be diluted in water. The powdered chemicals are the hardest to dissolve in water, so it's a good idea to mix them well ahead of time to give them plenty of time to dissolve. You can make a strong solution from the powder and then add more water at the time of use to dilute it to the proper level. Liquids can be kept in their original state until used and then diluted. The crystals usually dissolve quite readily, so they can also be prepared immediately before use.

Tap water is normally all right to use in making stains; but if your water is high in minerals, especially iron, it's best to use distilled water. Iron reacts with many of the chemicals to make a bluish-black stain.

If you want to be able to duplicate your results consistently, you should measure the amounts of chemicals and water that you mix. You can measure either by weight of dry chemical or by volume. A simple postal scale will be accurate enough for weighing the chemicals. To measure volume, you can use ordinary measuring cups or you can get a graduated flask at a chemical dealer or a company that sells photo darkroom supplies.

A gallon of chemical stain will cover about 600 square feet of wood.

Applying Chemical Stains

Most chemical stains are dissolved in water and applied in liquid form. One exception is ammonia fuming, where the chemical is applied as a vapor. To avoid raised grain in the final finish, the wood should be wet-sanded first, as is done for water stains. Use a chemical-resistant brush to apply the stains; nylon and polyester brushes are good for applying chemicals; of the natural filaments, tampico is probably the most chemical resistant.

Chemical stains must be applied evenly or streaks and blotches will appear in the finished surface. You can make it easier to get an even application by first brushing on a coat of clear water, then applying the stain while the water is still wet.

Fuming. Ammonia produces very strong fumes, as anyone who has used it knows. When these fumes settle on wood that is high in tannin, they will darken the color of the wood. Fumed oak used to be a very popular finish. Most antique oak furniture you see probably has been finished by fuming. The process of fuming is not widely used today, because it requires an airtight container large enough to accommodate the object being fumed and because ammonia is difficult to work with due to the strong fumes; but fuming has several advantages. It produces an even color without lap marks, streaks, or brush marks. It stains every surface of the object in one operation; and the fumes will even penetrate some finishes, so it is possible to change the color of a previously finished article without removing the old finish. The vapors penetrate deep into the wood, producing a color change that is more than just a surface coating. During the fuming process, no liquid comes in contact with the wood; so there is no problem of raised grain as there is with other chemical stains or water stain.

To fume a piece of wood, you must enclose it in an airtight container. This is not difficult for small items, but it can pose a problem if the item being finished is large. Larger items require that a special fuming box or tent be constructed. A wood box or crate with all joints sealed with caulking or tape will work. A fuming tent consists of framework of wood covered with plastic sheeting. Seal all of the joints with duct tape.

The best type of ammonia to use is 26 percent industrial ammonia. Household ammonia is much weaker; but it will work. It will just take longer. Pour some ammonia into several saucers and put the saucers into the container with the object to be stained. Seal up the container and let the ammonia fumes work on the wood for about 24 hours. The exact amount of time it takes will depend on the strength of the ammonia, the amount of tannin in the wood and the color you want to achieve. The colors produced by fuming range from light yellow through dark brown; a medium honey color is most common. The wood will darken slightly after it is allowed to air out.

Note: Wear a respirator when working with ammonia, and provide adequate ventilation.

Chemicals Used to Make Stains

The following list contains most of the chemicals commonly used to stain wood:

Tannic acid is the most basic ingredient in chemical staining. In woods like oak, walnut, and mahogany, the tannic acid or tannin is already present in the wood. Woods that are low in tannin require an application of tannic acid before some of the chemical stains will be effective. To make a solution for this purpose, mix five parts tannic acid with 95 parts water. Apply the solution to the work and let it dry before applying any other chemicals. *Tannic acid is toxic when eaten or inhaled.* Recently, tannic acid has been suspected of being a cancer-causing agent.

Strong tea is a safer substitute for tannic acid.

Ammonia reacts with tannin to produce a wide range of brown colors. Industrial strength ammonia produces the best results, but household ammonia can be used. It can be applied as a liquid or used in the fuming process. Ammonia has an advantage over other alkalis, because it completely evaporates from the wood. Other alkalis leave a residue that must be neutralized. *Breathing the concentrated fumes of ammonia may be fatal, so always provide adequate ventilation. There is a* moderate fire danger if ammonia fumes reach a point of 16 to 25 percent of the atmosphere.

Potash (potassium carbonate) produces results similar to ammonia. It comes as a powder that must be dissolved in water before use. It leaves a residue on the wood after it has dried. To remove the residue, wash with clean water, then neutralize it with a wash of household vinegar. Finally, wash with clean water again. Potash is a skin irritant.

Caustic soda (sodium hydroxide) is similar to potash in effect and must be neutralized in the same manner. *Caustic soda will burn the skin and is poisonous if swallowed.*

Potassium permanganate produces a wide range of beautiful browns when applied to high-tannin woods or over a wash of tannic acid. It comes in crystal form. Dissolve 1½ ounces of crystals into one quart of water for a medium brown. The solution will first turn the wood violet, but the color will change to brown as the wood dries. Potassium permanganate should always be used in a dilute solution; *this chemical may cause burns, and strong solutions can pose a fire risk.*

Potassium dichromate is similar to potassium permanganate except the color produced tends to be more yellowish. *This chemical is poisonous if inhaled or swallowed.* It may cause skin burns, and strong solutions can pose a fire risk.

Iron compounds are used to produce grey to black effects. Several coats may be necessary to make a deep black color similar to ebony. A light wash will give new wood the silver-grey color of weathered wood. The iron reacts with tannin so low-tannin woods should be treated with tannic acid before applying the iron compounds. Iron sulfate and iron chloride are commercially available iron compounds, but you can make your own iron stain by putting iron nails or iron filings into a jar of vinegar. Let the iron remain in the vinegar for several days. If you used filings, strain the mixture before applying it to the wood. Iron compounds will emphasize fancy grain patterns such as birds' eyes and crotch patterns; if they are applied in a weak solution, the grain will be enhanced without changing the basic wood color too much. There will be a slight greying of the wood, but a coat of water stain will hide the grey and still let the enhancement of the fancy pattern show.

Copper sulfate also produces a grey or black color when applied to wood. It is poisonous if swallowed.

Chemical Stain Formulas

Chemical stains offer a wide variation in color, depending on the strength of the solution used and the chemicals chosen, so they give you the opportunity to exert a lot of creative control over the staining process. But in order to use that creative control, you will need to experiment before the final formula is decided on. Here are a few formulas for simple stains:

Color: brown
Woods effective on: oak, walnut, chestnut, mahogany
Chemicals used: ammonia
Brush or sponge the ammonia onto the wood. Let dry. Repeat applications until color desired is achieved. The ammonia can also be applied by fuming.

Color: grey brown
Woods effective on: walnut, gum
Chemicals used: ammonia, copper sulfate.
Apply ammonia to the wood and let it evaporate. Mix one teaspoon of copper sulfate crystals with one cup of water. Brush the copper sulfate solution onto the wood and let dry. Adding additional coats of copper sulfate will darken the color. Thoroughly wash off the copper sulfate residue with water.

Color: ebony
Woods effective on: oak, walnut
Chemicals used: vinegar, iron filings
Add one ounce of iron filings to one quart of vinegar. The filings can be collected from a bench grinder used to sharpen tools. Iron nails can be used instead of the filings, but they may need to soak in the vinegar longer. Let the vinegar-iron mixture sit for about one week; it's ready when it looks grey and cloudy. Strain the mixture through a paint filter or several layers of cloth to remove the filings. Apply repeated coats of the vinegar mixture to the wood until a dark grey-black color is achieved; after a finish is applied, the color will be deep black.

Color: weathered grey
Woods effective on: oak
Chemicals used: iron sulfate
Apply a weak solution of iron sulfate to the wood and let it dry. Repeat the application if a darker grey is wanted.

Color: light brown
Woods effective on: birch, maple, pine, fir
Chemicals used: ammonia, tea
Make an extra-strong batch of tea. Brush the tea onto the wood and let dry. Apply ammonia to the wood either by brushing or by fuming.

Color: weathered grey
Woods effective on: birch, maple, pine, fir, oak
Chemicals used: iron filings and vinegar, tea
Brush strong tea onto the wood and let it dry. Make the iron-vinegar solution described earlier and apply it to the wood. Apply additional coats of the solution until the desired shade is reached.

10 · Gilding and Stencilling

Gilding and stencilling are both popular methods of decorating wood. Either of these techniques can turn an ordinary looking piece of furniture into something unique. Gilding is often used as an edge treatment or to accentuate decorative carvings. Stencilling is used to add decorative designs to the wood surface. The two techniques are used in combination to produce the gold stencilled designs commonly associated with Hitchcock chairs and Boston rockers.

GILDING

Gilding is the process of applying a metallic leaf or powder to the wood surface. The metal is usually gold or gold colored, but silver and copper colored metals are also used.

In the past, entire pieces of furniture were gilded; but the trend recently is to use gilding as an accent to highlight a shaped edge or a decorative carving. (Illus. 151)

Gold Leaf

Genuine gold leaf is made from 23½ carat gold that is beaten into thin sheets. Each sheet is less than one-thousandth of an inch thick. Because gold is expensive, imitation gold leaf is available. The imitation gold leaf is applied in the same manner as real gold leaf and looks quite real. It is made from a bronze alloy.

Illus. 151. This chest makes extensive use of gilding.

Because each leaf is so thin, it is difficult to handle it without tearing it. To keep the leaves from being damaged, they come in books usually containing 20 sheets. Each piece of gold leaf is sandwiched between the paper sheets of the book to protect the leaf. (Illus. 152) A special brush called a gilder's tip is used to remove the leaf from the book and apply it to the surface. A gilder's tip is a flat brush with a very thin layer of bristles. The gold leaf is attracted to the bristles by static electricity. Imitation gold leaf is a little more durable than the genuine gold, so it is sometimes possible to lift it by hand. Until you are proficient with the technique, it is best to practice with the imitation variety.

Surface preparation. The first step in preparing a piece of wood for gold leafing is to apply a coat of a substance called gesso. The gesso is very thick, so it fills any surface irregularities and provides a smooth base for the gold leaf. The traditional formula for a gesso is rabbitskin glue mixed with chalk powder. A more modern form of gesso uses an acrylic base. Some people prefer to substitute a coat of paint for the gesso. This is especially true if an antique effect is desired.

Illus. 152. Gold leaf comes in books with each piece sandwiched between sheets of paper to protect it.

When red paint is used as the base coat, the effect is frequently called Venetian gold. When the leaf is applied, tears in the leaf are allowed to remain uncovered, showing the red base. Black and brown paint are also frequently used in a similar fashion to get an antique look. Gold paint applied as the base coat will help to hide any tears or missed spots.

After the base coat is dry, the area to be gold-leafed is given a coat of adhesive size. The adhesive size may be thin rabbitskin glue, varnish, or a polyvinyl adhesive made specifically for the purpose. The polyvinyl adhesive is the easiest to use and is the most popular among beginners. Allow the size to dry until it is tacky. The polyvinyl size will be milky white when first applied and will slowly become transparent; when it is completely transparent, it is ready for the leaf to be applied.

Applying gold leaf. Open the book of gold leaf to the first page and touch the flat side of the gilder's tip to the leaf. The leaf will cling to the bristles of the gilder's tip. Lift the leaf from the page and press it into place on the adhesive size. Continue to apply the leaf in this manner until the entire area is covered. Each leaf should slightly overlap the previous one.

When all of the leaf has been applied, use a soft brush or a wad of soft cloth to press the gold leaf into all of the details of the surface. Next burnish the surface by gently rubbing a soft cloth over the gold leaf. The cloth will remove any pieces of leaf that overlap or are not attached firmly, leaving only a single layer of firmly attached gold leaf. If tears or missed spots appear at this stage, you can repair them by pressing a small piece of leaf into the defect. Burnish the leaf again to give it a smooth polished surface. Professional gilders use a special burnishing tool tipped with a piece of highly polished agate stone to complete the burnishing process.

Glazing. When an antique effect is desired, a glaze is applied over the gold leaf. The glaze is similar to thick stain. Oil or Japan tinting colors thinned with paint thinner make a good glaze. Glazes are usually colored with burnt umber, burnt sienna, or raw umber. Brush or wipe the glaze over the gold leaf and then use a soft cloth to highlight the glaze by wiping it off of the gold, leaving more glaze in the low spots and removing most of it from the high spots. Glazing is especially effective on carvings, because it shows off the detail.

Protective coating. After the glaze is dry or after the gold leaf is burnished and the size has dried, if no glaze is used, the leaf should be protected with a coat of varnish, lacquer, or a protective coating made specifically for gold leaf. Make sure that the coating is compatible with the gesso or base coat of paint, adhesive size, and the glaze. For example, if varnish was used as the size, it should also be used as the top coat; if lacquer is used as the top coat, it will react with the varnish below. The polyvinyl size can be used with any top coat.

Bronze Powder

Another method of gilding uses metallic powder to cover the surface. Although they are usually referred to as bronze powders, they are actually available in several colors that are made from different metals. Genuine gold as well as bronze, copper, silver and aluminum are frequently used to make gilding powder. You should use the finest grade of powder that you can get. The best type for this purpose is called bronze lining powder.

Applying bronze powder. The procedure for applying bronze powder is very similar to applying gold leaf. The surface should be sealed with a base coat of gesso or paint. Next, a coat of adhesive size should be applied. A special adhesive called bronzing liquid is available, but varnish or shellac are frequently used as the adhesive size. Let the adhesive size dry until it is tacky. Applying the bronze powder at the proper stage in the drying of the size is of extreme importance. If the size is too wet, the powder will gum up and smear; if the size is too dry, the powder won't adhere well. To test the size, press your finger onto an inconspicuous place; the size is just right when you hear a definite snap as you remove your finger. Don't attempt to cover too large an area at once or the size will dry before you can apply the powder to the entire surface.

Dip a small brush into the bronze powder and use it to pat the powder onto the surface. Don't brush the powder around; just gently apply it to the surface with a patting motion. At this point it is not necessary to entirely cover the surface with the powder. Next use a soft cloth to spread the powder around. Make sure that the surface has an even coat of bronze powder, then use the cloth to burnish the powder. Rub the cloth briskly over the powder to bring up a soft lustre.

You can glaze bronze powder in the same way that was described for gold leaf.

The final step is to apply a protective coat of varnish or lacquer.

Gilding Wax

Several companies market a gilding compound that consists of bronze powders mixed with a waxlike base. This is probably the easiest form of gilding available. No adhesive is needed. The gilding comes in a tube or a widemouth jar. To apply the gilding, simply rub it onto the surface with a piece of cloth. You can also thin the wax with paint thinner and apply it with a brush. Let it set for a few minutes, then burnish it with another cloth to bring up a smooth lustre. (Illus. 153)

You can glaze this type exactly the same way as the other types; but because of its unique method of application, you can

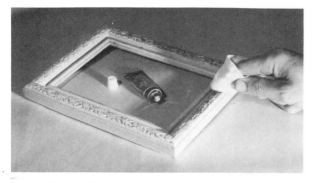

Illus. 153. Gilding wax is a good product to use when you want to highlight carvings such as those on this picture frame.

achieve the same results in a different manner. This technique is especially useful on intricate carvings where it is difficult to get the gilding into the low areas. Before applying any gilding, spray the entire carving with paint that is the same color as the glaze you would ordinarily use. When the paint is dry, use a cloth to wipe the gilding wax onto the high points of the carving, letting the paint show in the low areas. The resulting finish looks almost the same as if you had completely gilded the object and then glazed it, but it is much easier to achieve. Usually no protective coat is needed over the gilding wax, but items that will receive a lot of wear should be coated.

STENCILLING

When stencils are used to apply a decorative pattern to a piece of furniture, even an ordinary piece can be turned into a showpiece. The stencilling procedure is a simple one, but the results can be dramatic. Stencilling is usually associated with antique designs, but there is nothing in the process that limits it to antique reproductions; many modern patterns can be adapted to stencils.

Stencils can be used either with paint or bronze powders. The bronze powder method is used to reproduce the look of old Hitchcock chairs; colorful paints are more often used for modern or Pennsylvania Dutch patterns.

Choosing a Pattern

The first step in stencilling is choosing a pattern that will harmonize with the furniture you will apply it to. You can draw your own pattern or copy an antique pattern. Craft stores sell pattern books, and a trip to a museum will result in many ideas for antique patterns.

There are two main types of patterns: the single element pattern and the complex pattern. Single element stencils consist of only one element of a pattern, a leaf for example; several single element stencils can be used to make a design, or one single element stencil can be used over and over to make a repetitious design. A complex pattern stencil combines all of the elements of the design in a single stencil. The complex pattern stencil is easier to use but harder to make. The single element stencil offers more creative freedom, because you can vary the elements in a particular design without making a completely new stencil. Generally, single element stencils are only used with the bronze powder technique, because once the powder is applied it won't smear. Complex pattern stencils are used to apply paint, because the paint will smear if you keep applying different stencils over the same area.

Reproducing a Pattern

When you have chosen the pattern you want to use, you will usually need to enlarge or reduce it to fit the item to which you want to apply it. You can use several methods to do this. The easiest method is to use a photocopy machine that has reduction and enlargement capabilities. Simply place the original in the machine and set the machine for the appropriate amount of reduction or enlargement. If the pattern needs to vary more than about 50 percent in size, most copy machines won't do it in one step. To achieve a reduction or enlargement greater than the highest setting on the machine, simply make a copy with the machine set at its highest setting then remove the original and replace it with the copy. Make a new copy with the machine set for reduction or enlargement as needed. If the new copy still is not the correct size, put it in the original position and copy it again. You can continue in this manner until you have achieved the correct amount of reduction or enlargement. You will lose a little copy quality each time you make a copy of a copy; but since you will trace the outline off later, you only need to have a recognizable outline to produce a good stencil.

The grid method is another way to enlarge or reduce a pattern. It is more time consuming and requires more skill than the photocopy method. Start by drawing equally spaced grid lines over the original pattern, so that the pattern is covered with many small equally sized squares. Next you will need a piece of graph paper, or you will need to draw a second set of grid lines on another sheet of paper. If you want to enlarge the pattern, the second set of grid lines should be larger than the original ones you drew on the pattern. If you are reducing the pattern, the second set of grid lines should be smaller than the original. For example, if you want the final pattern to be half the size of the original, draw ½ in. squares on the original and ¼ in. squares on the second sheet of paper.

To transfer the pattern, you must draw the portion of the outline of the original that falls into one square into the corresponding square on the second sheet of paper. This is not as hard as it may sound. Because the squares are so small, the outline is broken up into very short segments that usually consist of straight or slightly curved lines. All that is necessary is to observe how that line is positioned in the square and draw it accordingly on the second sheet. If you are careful, this method will give you a faithful reproduction. The smaller the squares are on the original the more accurate the reproduction will be.

The third method of enlarging or reducing a pattern uses a machine called a pantograph. The pantograph consists of several wooden or metal arms that are pivoted on each other. Many pivot points are provided. Changing the pivot points alters the amount of reduction or enlargement. The original is secured to the table under the arm of the pantograph that has a stylus attached. A blank sheet of paper is secured under another arm of the machine that has a pen or pencil attached. As you trace around the outline of the original with the stylus, the machine will automatically reproduce the pattern on the other sheet of paper, enlarged or reduced depending on how you set the pivot points. You can buy a pantograph at an art supply store.

If you want to copy the pattern from an antique, but it would be difficult to physically trace the pattern onto a piece of tracing paper; you can take a photo of the pattern. Use slide film and hold the camera so that the film is parallel with the surface the pattern is applied to. If the camera is held at an angle, the pattern will be distorted. When the film is developed, you can project the slide with a slide projector. Tape a piece of paper to the wall and project the pattern onto it. Adjust the distance of the projector from the paper until the pattern is the correct size. Don't tilt the projector; mount the paper so that it's level with the projector lens. If the projector is tilted, the pattern will be distorted. Now simply trace around the projected image to reproduce it onto the paper.

Cutting a Stencil

Once the pattern is the correct size, transfer it to the stencil material using carbon paper. Stencils can be made from several materials. If the stencil will be used with bronze powder, it should be made of architect's linen which is available at drafting supply stores. Stencils for paint can be made of stencil paper which is made specifically for that purpose, or they can be made from the heavy manila paper used to make file folders. If the manila paper is used, a coat of shellac on both sides of the finished stencil will increase the life of the stencil. If you plan to reuse a stencil repeatedly, drafting acetate may prove to be more durable than either stencil board or manila paper. Stencils used for industrial production runs are usually made from thin sheets of copper, zinc, or aluminum.

To cut architect's linen, stencil board, manila paper, or acetate, you will need a razor knife. Almost any hobby knife will do; but for the best results, buy a frisket knife or a swivel knife. A frisket knife is used to cut masks for air brushing and is ideal for cutting stencils; a swivel knife is especially useful for cutting designs that have numerous curving lines. The blade of a swivel knife swivels in the handle, so you can follow a curved line without constantly twisting the knife handle. Both types are available at craft stores or drafting supply stores.

Place the stencil on a cutting board made of hardboard, to cut out the openings. Architect's linen has a dull side and a shiny side; cut the stencil with the dull side up. Some people prefer to work on a light table so that they can see that the cut has been made all the way through the paper. You will have more control of the knife if you draw it towards you. Continually reposition the paper so you can make all of the cuts in this manner. If you keep the knife sharp, very little pressure will be needed to cut through the paper, so there won't be much chance of slipping and cutting yourself. However, if you let the knife get dull, you will need to apply too much force and the chances of slipping and injuring yourself (or, at least, ruining the stencil) will be multiplied. You can keep the blade sharp by stropping it on a small piece of leather. If a little stropping won't make the blade acceptably sharp, replace the blade with a new one.

Any portion of the stencil that protrudes into a cutout area must be connected to the rest of the stencil. The connection is called a tie, if it is connected at both ends, or a wing, if it is connected only at one end. Wings should be avoided whenever possible, because they tend to lift up as the paint is applied, and blur the image; also they are easier to tear off, so the stencil won't last as long. Take care as you cut close to a tie; if you nick the tie, it will be weakened and won't last as long.

Stencils made of sheet metal are cut differently. Sandwich the sheet metal between two pieces of ¼-in.-thick wood. Secure the pieces together with nails or screws driven through waste areas. Transfer the pattern to one of the boards. Use a jigsaw or a coping saw to cut out the pattern. Drill an entry hole for the blade in each opening of the pattern. Metal stencils can be designed exactly like paper stencils, but if you would like to eliminate all ties from the design, metal stencils offer an advantage. You can cut all of the portions of the stencil that would normally need to be attached with ties as separate pieces, then use small pieces of wire soldered to the back of the stencil to secure them in their proper position. Because the wires won't touch the wood surface, the ties won't show in the final design. This method is especially useful for stencils that will be used with spray paint.

Bronze Powder Stencilling

Bronze powder stencilling is one of the most impressive types of furniture decoration, and it is a technique which offers you a lot of creative control. The famous original Hitchcock chairs that were made in the mid-1800's used this form of decoration.

The reason there is so much creative con-

Illus. 154. Bronze powder stencilling can produce a shaded effect as seen in this stencilled pear.

trol with this technique is that the process allows you to blend different colors of bronze powders in the same stencil, and you can shade the design by varying the amount of powder applied to give it a three-dimensional quality. (Illus. 154) Single element stencils can easily be combined into complex designs using this technique, so you can vary the design to suit the shape of the article it is applied to. In this way, several different pieces of furniture can be unified into a set by using common design elements, and yet the actual design can be varied to suit the individual piece.

To show off the bronze powder, the background must be dark; most original antiques were painted black, but the trend today is to use a dark stain so the wood grain will still show.

The first step in applying a bronze powder stencil is to give the area that will receive the stencil a thin coat of slow-drying varnish. Let the varnish dry until it is hard but still tacky. If you press your finger against the varnish and then pull it away, you should hear a sharp snap if the varnish has reached the proper stage of dryness. Also, there should not be a noticeable depression made in the varnish by your finger. It may take anywhere

from ten minutes to one hour for the varnish to reach this point, depending on the room temperature and humidity; so test the varnish about every ten minutes.

Apply the architect's linen stencil glossy side down to the varnished surface. If the varnish is at the proper stage of tackiness, the stencil will stick to the surface and yet it won't leave a mark when it is removed. You need to work quickly at this point, because the varnish will continue to dry and will soon lose its tack.

Bronze powder comes in many colors. As you become more proficient with this technique, you may want to try many different shades; but at first you can achieve good results using the following colors: aluminum, pale gold, rich gold, and extra brilliant fire. A piece of velvet cloth glued to a square of cardboard makes a good palette for the powders. Fold the cardboard in half so it can be closed like a book for storage. Apply a small quantity of each color powder in a spot on the palette. Wrap a small piece of smooth soft chamois or cloth around your index finger and rub it into the color you desire on the palette; only a little powder is needed, so wipe the excess onto the palette. Now rub your finger over the cut-out stencil area. (Illus. 155) Rub harder where you want a

Illus. 155. To spread the bronze powder, wrap a piece of chamois or a soft cloth over the end of your finger; dip your finger into the bronze powder and rub it over the area to be stencilled.

highlight, and apply very little pressure in the shaded areas. By using this procedure, you can give a three-dimensional look to the work. You may need to use a small artist's brush to apply the powder to very small details like leaf stems. Make sure that all of the bronze powder is rubbed into the varnish or removed from the area with a clean cloth, then remove the stencil. The same stencil can be reapplied in another area or a new one can be used to build up the design. If you use the same stencil over again, be sure there isn't any bronze powder clinging to it or it may leave a smudge when you reapply it. It's all right if the edge of a stencil overlaps an area that has already been stencilled, because the powder won't smudge once it has been rubbed into the varnish.

If the varnish loses its tack before you finish, let it dry for 24 hours then revarnish it and continue working. Be sure to remove any stray bronze powder before you revarnish. Stray powder can usually be removed by washing the area with a mild soap solution; stubborn areas can be removed by rubbing with a pencil eraser. You can heighten the three-dimensional quality of bronze stencilling by applying a second coat of varnish over the first set of design elements and then applying more portions of the design slightly overlapping the first elements. The coat of varnish between the two designs will create a three dimensional appearance as the design is viewed from different angles.

When the stencilling is done and the varnish is dry, apply two coats of varnish over the design to protect it.

Paint Stencilling

Pennsylvania Dutch patterns and modern patterns usually look better if colored paint is used rather than bronze powder. Stencils used with paint are usually of the complex pattern type where all of the design elements are cut into one stencil; this is because it is difficult to apply several stencils to the same area without smearing the paint. Painted stencils can be applied either before or after the last coat of finish has been applied. The finishing materials under the stencil should be completely dry before the paint is applied. Use masking tape to hold the stencil in place. Spraying is probably the easiest way to apply paint to a stencil. Aeresol cans work well; hold the can a little farther away from the work than normal and spray straight at the work, not at an angle. If you spray at an angle, the paint can be forced under the edge of the stencil. An air brush is an excellent way to apply the paint. The air brush gives you enough control to shade the stencil in a way similar to what you can do with bronze powder. Be sure to mask off any areas of the work that could be damaged by paint overspray.

Paint can also be applied with a brush. Any thick-bodied paint will work. A special stencilling brush looks like an old shaving brush, but the bristles are much stiffer and cut square on the end. An old paint brush can be adapted for use as a stencilling brush

Illus. 156. A stencilling brush resembles a shaving brush, but the bristles are stiffer. Dip the brush into a shallow dish of paint so that only the tips of the bristles have paint on them. Apply the paint by tapping the brush in an up and down stippling motion.

by cutting the bristles off so that only about one inch remains.

Pour a small amount of the paint onto a flat plate and dip the end of the brush into the paint. Only the very tip of the brush should have paint on it. Tap the brush on a piece of newspaper to remove any excess paint; then using a stippling motion, tamp the paint over the stencil, holding the brush square so that only the tips of the bristles touch the work. (Illus. 156)

If you want to use more than one color paint with the stencil, mask off all of the openings except those that will receive the first color. After applying the first color mask off those openings and remove the masking from the openings that will receive the second color. Any number of colors can be added using this method.

After all of the paint has been applied to the stencil, hold your hand on the stencil to prevent it from moving; and remove the masking tape with your other hand. Lift one corner of the stencil while holding down the opposite corner with your other hand. Peel the stencil off without any side to side movement that might smear the paint. Do this while the paint is still wet because the longer the stencil is in place, the greater the chance that the paint will bleed under the edge and create a fuzzy outline. If the paint is allowed to dry, the stencil will be glued to the surface by any paint that did bleed under the edge.

Clean the stencils with the appropriate paint thinner and save them for reuse.

Gold Leaf Stencilling

Gold leaf can be applied to a stencilled pattern. The process is similar to applying paint, only varnish is used instead. Remove the stencil and let the varnish dry until it is tacky. Apply the gold leaf to the varnished area in the usual manner; don't bother trying to follow the pattern, just cover the entire area with leaf. As you burnish down the gold leaf, it will only stick to the areas that re-ceived varnish through the stencil. Brush off all of the loose gold leaf and the original stencilled pattern will be perfectly reproduced in gold leaf.

Silk Screen Stencils

Silk screening is a process commonly associated with printing, but it can be used to apply decorations to wood. The process uses an open-mesh cloth that is specially made for the purpose, stretched over a frame that is open in the center. A liquid similar to lacquer is painted onto the cloth to close the openings in the cloth and prevent paint from going through. The open areas of the stencil are left untreated. It is possible to produce very complex patterns using the silk screen method, and this method eliminates the need for ties and wings so the design doesn't have that characteristic stencil look; it looks more like a freehand painted design. There is even a special emulsion that can be applied to the screen to make it light sensitive, so that designs can be applied photographically. With the photographic process, shading can be achieved by a process called halftoning, which superimposes a series of dots over the design. The dots are smaller in the light areas and larger in the dark areas.

Special silk screen paints must be used with this process. A quantity of paint is poured into one side of the frame and then the screen is placed onto the work; a rubber squeegee is used to scrape the paint from one side to the other, forcing paint through the open areas of the screen and onto the wood. Then the screen is lifted from the work, and it is ready to be applied to another piece. This method is well suited for limited production runs, because the screen can be immediately reused without any cleaning between applications. Enough paint can be kept in the frame to do several pieces before additional paint is needed. At the end of a run, the screen can be cleaned and saved for reuse or the design can be completely removed with a special solvent and the screen reused for a different design.

The best way to get started in silk screening is to buy a complete kit at a store that sells craft or drafting equipment. The kit will contain small quantities of all of the necessary supplies plus detailed directions; once you have become familiar with the materials in the kit, you will know which ones you use the most and you can buy them in larger quantities.

11 · Reproducing Antique Finishes

As genuine antiques become scarcer and more expensive, there is an increasing demand for antique reproductions. There are many degrees of authenticity in reproducing antique finishes; in some cases it is only necessary for the piece to have an antique look. At the other end of the scale is the exact duplicate which requires that the finish not only look old, it must be made of exactly the correct materials to correspond with the time period of the furniture style. Before attempting an exact duplicate, you need to thoroughly research the materials and techniques available at the time the original was built. Even the wood used is important; the best duplicates use old wood salvaged from old buildings or damaged furniture. However, in most cases an exact duplicate is not needed; you can use modern finishing materials as long as they are applied in a way that makes the piece look antique. (Illus. 157)

DISTRESSING

A genuine antique acquires a certain amount of damage during its hundreds of years of existence. If the damage is not severe, the marks left add to the piece's value because they denote its age. The process of purposely damaging a new piece of furniture to simulate these age marks is called distress-ing. The process has become a popular finish in its own right, and many new pieces of furniture are given a distressed finish. In many cases, there is no attempt to duplicate genuine distress marks. The surface is covered with marks that give it an interesting pattern, but bear no relation to the marks acquired over the years by a genuine antique.

Illus. 157. A distressed finish gives this piece an antique look.

If you want to duplicate a genuine antique, you should study several and try to analyze how the distress marks occurred. For example, many old chairs have distinctive marks around the bottoms of the front legs. These marks were made by riding spurs on the boots of men who sat in the chairs. Once you realize that these marks were left by spurs, you can see that it would be uncharacteristic to make similar marks on the upper portions of the chair. The writing surface of a desk may have many ink spots, but a cupboard probably wouldn't have any. Burn marks bear the shape of the object that made them; the marks should be consistent with the purpose the furniture was used for. Tables and cupboards used around a kitchen will bear the marks of hot pans, irons, or fireplace pokers; furniture used in other areas would be more likely to be burned by candles, lanterns, and cigarettes, cigars, and pipes. Since cigarettes came into widespread use fairly recently in the life of an antique, cigarette burns are not indicative of great age; an old clay pipe would be more appropriate.

There are two methods of applying distress marks: physical distressing and surface distressing. The most important thing to keep in mind when using either of these techniques is to make the marks appear random and naturally placed and not to overdo it. A little distressing can make a new piece look like a genuine antique; too much and it will look like a piece of junk.

Physical Distressing

To physically distress a piece of furniture, different objects are used to make actual dents, holes, burns, and scratches in the wood surface. If you are trying to make a close replica of a real antique, these marks should be applied after the finish is complete as would occur in real use; the marks left should then be filled with accumulations of dirt and wax (rottenstone mixed with paste wax makes a good substitute). Normally,

though, distressing is performed before the object is stained; this way the marks accumulate more stain than the rest of the surface and show up darker, and yet they are the same color and so they blend with the finish better.

Dents and scratches. The most common types of distress marks are dents and scratches; they are produced by hitting the wood with various metal objects. When you are trying for authenticity, you should use objects that would normally be found in a house of the correct time period to make physical distress marks. For example, use real spurs to make spur marks and use keys and kitchen utensils of the time period to dent table tops. If you are only after an antique look, the process is simpler. Attach several different metal objects like keys, bolts, nuts, nails, and screws to a length of chain and whip the wood surface with it.

Worm holes. An awl can be used to simulate worm holes in the wood, but real worm holes don't taper like the hole left by an awl. A more realistic worm hole can be made by driving a small brad into the wood and then removing it. Worm holes usually are at an angle rather than straight in.

Burn marks. A soldering iron or a woodburner can be used to make burn marks on the wood. Any metal object can be heated with a propane torch and then set on the wood surface to make a burn mark. Because of the danger of fire, propane torches should only be used outdoors. For authentic looking marks, take into consideration how the piece was used and then choose an object that would be appropriate to burn the wood. One characteristic type of burn mark is made when a coal oil lamp is placed too close to an upright part of a piece of furniture; the heat radiated from the glass of the lamp makes a burn that has no definite outline, but simply darkens the wood in a circular area. The best way to duplicate this type of burn is to place a kerosene lamp or a camping lantern in the proper position and let it burn the wood just as it would have happened a hundred years ago.

Worn edges.   Edges and corners receive more wear than other parts of a piece of furniture. You can simulate this wear by rasping and filing the edges round; worn edges naturally take on a highly polished look, so you should sand the rounded edges extremely smooth. Six-hundred grit sandpaper lubricated with a little paste wax will give the edges the proper polish. If you use wax, the sanding must be done after the finish has been applied. This produces a more authentic look anyway, because wear would normally remove the finish from the edges.

Animal marks.   Most antiques will have received at least a few scratches from the family pet over the years. These marks generally occur around the legs. If you have a dog or cat, you can probably persuade it to give the piece you're working on a few swipes with its claws; but if you can't, a piece of soup bone sharpened to a point will make realistic marks.

Surface Distressing

Surface distress marks are simply painted onto the surface of the wood; they are meant to simulate the spills and spots that accumulate over the years. Usually surface distressing is done after the stain is applied and before the top coats.

Fly specks.   Whenever a fly lands on something, it usually leaves behind a small brown spot. In a normally well-kept house today, there aren't many flies, and so there are few noticeable fly specks on the furniture; but in earlier days, flies were much more common in houses and antique furniture has had hundreds of years to accumulate flies, so most antiques are covered with a fairly uniform coating of small dots. Many people today don't even know what causes these spots, but they have become a trademark of an antique finish.

Fly specks are easy to duplicate; although the real thing is brown, black paint is usually used to simulate them. One method uses a stiff brush like the kind used to spread soldering flux. Dip the brush into some thick paint then brush across the bristles with a stick. This will send a shower of small droplets spraying from the brush. Continue to spray the droplets over the wood surface until you are are satisfied with the results.

You can also use spray equipment or an aerosol can to make fly specks. Adjust the spray gun until it sprays out small droplets instead of an atomized spray. Usually you can accomplish this with a combination of low air pressure, thick paint, and a fairly heavy feed adjustment. If you press the valve of an aerosol can down only part way, it will sputter and spray out droplets that also simulate fly specks.

Of course, if you are after the ultimate in authenticity, only the real thing will do. Store the completed piece of furniture in a barn or stable where flies congregate. If there are enough flies, you can get several hundred years worth of specks in a few months.

Ink spots.   Desk tops are usually covered with at least a few ink spots. Use India ink to make the spots. A drawing pen can be used to make small spots that simulate areas where ink soaked through a page or where the pen slipped off the paper. Ink spills are made by simply pouring a little ink onto the surface. If you would like something unique, draw an impressive looking signature on a piece of paper with India ink; and while the ink is still wet, place the paper upside down on the wood and rub across the back. The result will be a reverse impression of the signature on the wood, as if a document was turned over on the desk without being blotted.

Spills.   Various types of food and drink spills can be duplicated by mixing a small amount of watercolor in water and pouring the water onto the wood. Let the water dry without disturbing it. If you want a glass ring, pour a little of the mixture on the wood and set a glass into the puddle; then leave it alone until the water dries.

Random marks.   If you would like an antique looking finish without really duplicating any particular mark, you can achieve a good effect by daubing various objects into the wet stain as you stain the wood. Oil stain works best; wipe it as usual, but leave a little more wet stain on the surface than you normally would. Take a crumpled-up newspaper or a sponge and daub it into the wet stain. If you aren't satisfied with the marks, you can wipe them out with a rag and try again.

STAINS

Any modern stain will provide satisfactory results if you aren't trying for an exact duplicate. Water stains and NGR (non-grain-raising) stains are especially good. Refer to Chapter 5 for directions on custom-mixed stains, if you are trying to match a particular color.

If you want to duplicate an antique finish, you have to use stains that were available to the finisher at the time the original pieces were built. Most antiques were stained with either vegetable stains or chemical stains.

Vegetable stains.   Vegetable stains are natural substances derived from various plants, roots, nuts, berries, bark, and leaves. The resulting stains behave much like modern aniline dye water stains.

Probably the most widely used vegetable stain is made from walnut husks. As a walnut grows on the tree, it is covered with a soft green husk; as the nuts mature, this husk turns dark brown. When the nuts are harvested, the husk is removed, revealing the nut shell underneath. To make a stain from the husks, put them in a pot that has no exposed metal; an enamelled steel pot or a pot with a nonstick coating will work, or use an earthenware container. Cover the husks with water and add a small amount of caustic soda (a tablespoon to a gallon of water). Simmer the mixture over low heat for several days. If you don't want to keep the mixture on the stove that long, try simmering it for a few hours, then put the mixture into a clear glass container tightly capped; and let it sit in bright sunlight for about a week. After the water has taken on the dark brown color of the husks, strain the liquid through several layers of cloth. If you make a large batch, you can store the mixture in bottles and have a supply to last several years. You can dilute this stain to produce a wide range of brown colors; deeper colors can be achieved by applying several coats of the stain. Some companies still supply this type of stain in a dry crystal form called walnut extract crystals.

The following is a list of other plant substances that were used as dyes; they are made into stain in approximately the same way as the walnut husk stain. Some may not require as long a simmering time:

Campeachy wood: Its extract is called logwood extract; color is black or grey; can be changed to brown, violet or blue by treating the dried stain with various chemical stains such as ammonia, iron and vinegar, or copper sulfate.

Brazil-wood: Simmer shavings in water with a touch of caustic soda. Produces a variety of reds and reddish browns.

Chicory root: Simmer the roasted roots in

water for about one hour. The color is yellowish brown.

Tea: Make a strong brew, add a pinch of caustic soda. Color is golden brown.

Coffee: Make a strong brew; add pinch of caustic soda. Color is warm brown.

Tobacco: Simmer a plug of chewing tobacco in water with a pinch of caustic soda for several hours. Makes a brown-colored stain.

Alkanet root: Soak in mineral oil; leave in warm sun for several days. Red in color.

Some other vegetable stains were made from the following: dragon's blood (red), chestnut (brown), madder (purplish red), cochineal (red), yellow wood (yellow to olive brown), quercitron (yellow).

Chemical stains. Chemical stains have been used for years. Chapter 9 gives complete directions for using chemical stains. Chemical stains were often used in conjunction with vegetable stains. Sometimes the chemical stain was applied first, then a vegetable stain applied over it to deepen or alter the color. In other cases a chemical stain was applied over the vegetable stain to alter its color. Since the vegetable stains are basically the same colorants found in natural wood, the chemical stains react with them in about the same way. So you can expect ammonia to add more of a brownish cast to a vegetable stain, while iron compounds will give the stain a grey or black look. Experimentation is the only way to determine the exact effect.

GLAZES

After the stain has been applied, a glaze is sometimes used to heighten the antique look. A glaze is similar to a pigmented oil stain; you can make your own by following the directions in Chapter 5 for mixing your own stains, or you can buy a readymade stain or antiquing ink. Usually the glaze is a shade darker than the first stain used. Apply the glaze to the entire surface, then wipe it off of all of the raised surfaces, leaving it only in the dents, cracks, and crevices. The glaze simulates years of accumulated wax and dirt.

FINAL COATS

After the piece has been distressed and the stain applied, the only thing left to do is apply the final coats of protective finish. For a really authentic looking job, you should use a finish that fits the period. Four popular finishes used on antique furniture are wax, linseed oil, shellac, and varnish.

Wax

A wax finish is one of the simplest to apply, so it was widely used on antique furniture. Wax is not too durable, so it is not as widely used today. To make an antique wax, use a plane to cut shavings off of a block of beeswax. Pour turpentine over the shavings and let them soak until they are completely dissolved. The resulting mixture should be the consistency of thick paint. Rub the wax onto the wood with a cloth and let it dry, then buff it with a soft cloth. Several coats are usually needed. This formula works well for closed-grain woods; but on open-grained wood like oak, the wax will accumulate in the pores and eventually turn white. To combat this, the oldtime finishers added lamp black or burnt umber to the wax. Black wax was frequently used over a fumed oak finish. The black wax in the pores accentuates the pore pattern.

You can produce a similar finish that is more durable by using a modern paste type furniture wax. Universal tinting colors can be added to this type of wax to produce black or brown wax.

Linseed Oil

Boiled linseed oil has been used as a finish

for years. The modern penetrating oil finishes are easier to use and are more durable. They look very similar, so in most cases you can substitute a modern penetrating oil finish. If you want to apply a genuine linseed oil finish, follow this old finishing adage: Apply the oil once an hour for a day, once a day for a week, once a week for a year, and once a year for the rest of your life. What this adage is really saying is that it takes a lot of coats of linseed oil to make a good finish. Apply the oil with a rag; let it soak into the wood for about half an hour, then buff it off with a clean rag.

Shellac

Shellac is a very old finish. Until recently, it was considered to be one of the very finest finishes; so most really good antiques are finished with shellac. The shellac was almost always applied by French polishing (see Chapter 4). White shellac is a rather recent development, so antiques should always be finished with either button shellac or orange shellac.

Varnish

Today's natural oil varnishes are similar to those used on antiques, so you can get a good approximation of an antique varnish finish by using them.

Varnish tends to darken over the years; to simulate this, you can add oil tinting colors to the varnish.

Sometimes old varnish becomes brittle and the surface becomes covered with thousands of tiny hairline cracks. This is hard to duplicate, but there are several methods you can try. Craft stores sell a type of varnish that cracks as it drys; the cracks produced aren't exactly like the naturally occurring ones, but this is a sure way to get a cracked finish if you want one. You can experiment with some other methods, but the results are not always consistent. One way is to apply one coat of a long oil varnish like spar varnish, then apply a coat of short oil rubbing varnish while the first coat is still tacky. If you're lucky, the top coat will dry to a brittle finish before the first coat is dry. As the first coat dries, it will cause the top coat to crack. Subjecting the finish to heat or cold may enhance the cracking. Another method is to apply water-based varnish over the tacky spar varnish.

The most realistic cracks can be produced by applying a coat of spar varnish and letting it dry. Then apply a coat of the hardest short oil varnish you can find. Let the varnish dry and hope for the best. It may take several years for the cracks to develop. Subjecting the finish to changes in temperature and humidity may hasten the process.

Milk Paint

Most antiques that were painted received a coating of milk paint. Milk paint has a very characteristic look that doesn't resemble modern paints. The colors are usually muted and faded looking, because natural earth pigments were used.

Some manufacturers now make a powdered milk paint that follows the old formula. They use the same type of pigments originally used, so they look very authentic. To prepare this type of milk paint for use, you only need to add water. These commercial milk paints are usually the best bet; they look authentic, they are easy to use and they give uniform results. Mixing your own milk paint is a little harder and the results aren't guaranteed; but if you want to try making your own milk paint, here is one formula:

For a small batch mix two cups slaked lime (also called hydrated lime. Don't use quicklime; it generates heat when mixed with water) with one-half cup water. Let the lime soak up the water for several hours. Add one pint of plain cottage cheese to the lime and let it stand until all of the lumps are dissolved. Thin to the desired consistency by adding skim milk.

If you want a color other than white, be sure to use tinting colors that are compatible with lime; some types may produce a chemical reaction. Use dry powdered colors that aren't mixed with any vehicle. Here is a list of some colors that are compatible with lime: ferric oxide (indian red), ultramarine blue, cobalt blue, precipitated yellow iron oxide, copper phthalocyanine green, sienna, ochre.

GLOSSARY

abrasive cloth   A coated abrasive with a cloth backing. Emery cloth is an example.

acrylic   A man-made resin used in paints and other finishing products. Most commonly used in water-emulsion paints and varnishes.

adhesive size   Adhesive used to apply gold leaf or bronze powder. Rabbitskin glue, varnish, or polyvinyl adhesive are frequently used for this purpose.

airless spray equipment   Spray equipment that uses a hydraulic pump to pressurize liquid instead of using compressed air.

alkali   A chemical that will neutralize an acid. Strong alkali can burn skin. Referred to in chemistry as a "base."

alkyd   A synthetic resin frequently used in oil-based paint.

alligatoring   Numerous cracks in a paint film. The pattern of cracks resembles alligator skin. Caused by inflexibility in the paint, too heavy a build-up of old coats of paint, incompatibility between paint and primer or improper surface preparation.

aluminum oxide   A synthetic abrasive used as the cutting agent on sandpaper and other coated abrasives. The most desirable all-around abrasive for wood finishing. It is produced in an electric furnace.

aniline dye   A synthetic colorant used extensively in the manufacture of wood stains. It may be formulated to dissolve in oil, water, or alcohol. It is especially well suited for stains because of its permanence and because it is transparent.

annual rings   Growth rings of a tree caused by the variation in growth rate between spring and summer. Summerwood is denser and darker in color than springwood. Also called "annular rings."

aught system   A system of grading different sizes of abrasive particles for use in coated abrasives. Most grades useful for wood finishing are designated by several zeros (aughts), the more zeros the finer the abrasive. Grade 0 (also written 1/0) corresponds to a medium grit, 00000 (5/0) is very fine. Coarser grits are designated by numbers that get larger as the grit gets coarser. Grade 1 is coarse and grade 4 is very coarse. This system has largely been supplanted by the more accurate mesh system.

backing   The material that abrasive particles are attached to in coated abrasives. Paper, cloth, and fibreboard are common backings.

binders   Another name for resins used in paint. *See* resin.

black sable   A natural filament used for lettering and striping brushes.

bleeding   A paint defect that occurs when natural colors in wood seep (bleed) through the paint film making a stain on the paint surface.

blistering   A paint defect caused by moisture trapped beneath the paint surface. The moisture breaks the bond between the paint and the wood, lifting the paint film into a blister. It is the result either of interior moisture from a house or painting in direct sunlight which causes the film of the paint to dry before the undercoating.

block cushion grainer   A wood-graining tool used to mechanically reproduce wood grains. It has a rubber face that is covered with concentric, semi-circular grooves.

blond shellac   A highly refined grade of shellac that is light amber in color.

boiled linseed oil   Oil derived from the seed of the flax plant. The raw oil is not boiled but heated and driers are added. It is a major ingredient of a variety of finishing products.

bristle   Any natural filament used in brush manufacture. In common usage can describe any type of filament, either natural or synthetic, used in a brush.

brush marks   Parallel ridges left by a brush in a brushed-on coating.

burn-in stick   A type of filler used to repair defects in finished wood surfaces. They come in a variety of colors to match the existing finish. A heated knife is used to apply the filler. Also called shellac stick or lacquer stick.

burnished surface   A surface that has a smooth, polished look.

button shellac   The least refined grade of shellac. It is a dark brown color.

cambium   A layer of cells just beneath the bark of a tree where new growth occurs.

camel hair   A natural filament used to make brushes for use with lacquers and water colors.

catalyst   A chemical that speeds up a reaction between other chemicals. When catalysts are mixed with certain resins like polyester or epoxy, they cause the resin to harden into a solid plastic.

chalking   A dusty film of pigments left on the surface of weathered paint.

chemical stains   Stains that rely on a chemical reaction with natural chemicals in the wood to produce a color change.

china wood oil   *See* tung oil.

chroma   Color intensity.

closed-coat sandpaper   Sandpaper that has the entire surface of the backing covered with abrasive particles. It cuts fast but clogs easily.

closed-grain   Wood with no easily discernible pore structure. Does not require filling to achieve a smooth finish.

coated abrasives   Any product made by attaching abrasive particles to a backing. Sandpaper, abrasive cloth, and sanding belts are all coated abrasive products.

cold finish   A finish that uses solvents that don't dissolve most other types of finishes. Cold finishes can be safely applied over most previously finished surfaces. Varnish is a cold finish. *See* hot finish.

complementary colors   Colors opposite each other on the color wheel. Mixing complementary colors with each other decreases the intensity of their color and makes them more greyish.

cooked oil   Tung oil that has been heat-treated.

crazing   Thousands of tiny interconnecting cracks that can occur in a finish.

cut   The relationship between the weight of dry flakes and the volume of solvent used in making shellac. A one-pound cut consists of one pound of dry shellac flakes dissolved in one gallon of solvent.

danish oil   A penetrating oil finish made from a mixture of oils, driers, resins and solvents. It is generally easier to use than pure tung oil.

denatured alcohol   Ethyl alcohol that has been made undrinkable by the addition of poisonous substances. Also called proprietary solvent. It is used as a solvent for shellac.

distressing   The process of intentionally damaging a finish to give it an antique look.

dryers   Chemicals added to finishing products to speed up the drying process.

dust nibs   Tiny bumps in a finished surface caused by dust particles landing on the wet finish.

edge-grain wood   A term applied to quarter-sawed wood, particularly softwood. *See* quarter-sawed.

emery   A natural mineral used for coated abrasives. One of the harder natural abrasives.

end grain   A wood surface that has been cut at a 90° angle to the length of the cells, often the end of a piece of lumber. End grain absorbs finishing material to a greater degree than other wood surfaces because open-cell cavities are exposed at the surface.

epoxy   A synthetic resin used in paints and varnishes. It is extremely hard and wear-resistant. It is usually used with a catalyst.

extenders   Inert ingredients added to paint to improve its working characteristics. Also called "suspenders" or "fillers."

exterior protective stain   Stain specifically formulated to protect exterior wood as well as color it. No additional protective top coat is needed when this type of stain is used.

ferrule   The metal band that attaches the filaments to the handle of a brush.

filament   A slender fibre or hair used in a brush, commonly called a bristle.

filler stick   A type of wax-based wood putty in stick form. It comes in a variety of colors. Frequently used to fill nail holes after a finish has been applied.

filling   The process of packing the pores of open-grained wood with filler to create a smooth surface.

fish eyes   Small, round depressions in a finished surface. Frequently caused by contamination of the finish with silicones.

flagging   Split ends at the tips of brush filaments.

flat   A finished surface with no gloss.

flat-grain wood   Another name for plain-sawed wood, particularly softwood. *See* plain-sawed.

flex   When applied to coated abrasives, flex refers to a pattern of pre-bent lines in the backing. Flex increases the life of a coated abrasive by making it more able to withstand repeated bending.

flint   A natural mineral abrasive used to make sandpaper. It is rather soft compared to synthetic abrasives.

flitch   The log, or portion of log, from which veneers are cut. Also a stack of veneers all cut from the same log and laid in the order in which they were cut.

foam brush   A brush that substitutes a single piece of spongelike plastic foam for the individual filaments of a standard brush.

french polishing   The process of applying shellac with a pad in a series of steps.

garnet   A natural mineral abrasive used as the cutting agent in coated abrasives. It is the most desirable of the natural abrasives for woodwork.

glaze   A heavy-bodied stain used to give an antique look to gold leaf, bronze powder, and wood finishes.

glazing   The process of applying a glaze. Also the process of spraying a darker stain around the edge of a panel, door, or drawer front.

gloss   Finishes designated as gloss or high gloss dry to a smooth, shiny, reflective surface. The opposite of gloss is flat.

grain   The pattern produced by the annual rings in a piece of wood. Grain also refers to the direction of the wood fibres. For example, "sanding with the grain" means moving the sandpaper in strokes that parallel the length of the wood fibres.

graining   The process of applying a finish that looks like grained wood.

graining comb   A tool used to simulate the straight parallel grain typical of quarter-sawed wood. It has many closely spaced teeth similar to a hair comb.

graining stain   A heavy-bodied stain used in wood graining. Several types of stains are used but they all are thick and resist flowing once it has been applied.

grit   Abrasive particles used in coated abrasives. The term is often used when referring to the grade (coarseness) of an abrasive.

ground coat   The base coat for graining. The ground coat is colored to match the lightest color in the wood that is being imitated.

hardwood   Wood derived from broad-leafed trees. The term has no relation to the actual hardness of the wood. *See* softwood.

heartwood   Wood from the center portion of the log. It is generally darker and more decay-resistant than the younger sapwood.

horsehair   A natural filament used in brushes. It is usually blended with other filaments. When the percentage of horsehair in a brush becomes too large the quality of the brush is degraded.

hot finish   A finish that contains solvents that will attack other finishes. Lacquer is a hot finish. Hot finishes should not be applied over cold finishes. *See* cold finish.

hue   Technical name for what is commonly simply referred to as "color."

japan colors   Colored pigments mixed with a vehicle that is compatible with either oil or lacquer-based products. It comes as a thick paste that must be thinned before mixing it with other products.

japan dryer   A mixture of driers and solvents that speeds up the drying process of oil-based products. Generally not recommended for addition to modern finishing products, but it is used when making your own stains.

knot   The intersection between a limb and the trunk of a tree that shows up in sawed lumber as a round, oval, or spike-shaped area that is darker and harder than the surrounding wood. A "tight knot" is firmly attached to the surrounding wood. A "loose knot" has a layer of bark between it and the surrounding wood and may eventually fall out leaving a hole in the board. The grain pattern changes sharply around a knot, making it difficult to plane.

lacquer   A tough, fast-drying finish that contains very strong solvents. Lacquer is called a "hot finish" because the solvents it contains will dissolve most other finishes. For this reason lacquer should not be applied directly on top of an old finish other than lacquer. It is usually applied by spraying, but brushing lacquers are available.

latex stain   A water-based stain that behaves like oil-based pigmented stain. It should not be confused with water stain which uses transparent dyes to stain the wood.

lignin   The natural glue that holds wood fibres together.

linseed oil   Oil derived from flaxseed. The raw oil will not dry. "Boiled" linseed oil has had driers added to make it dry.

long oil varnish   Varnish that contains 40–100 gallons of oil per 100 pounds of resin. The large amount of oil makes the film tough, durable and elastic, but it is not suitable for rubbed finishes and it dries to only a moderate gloss. It is mostly used for exterior applications.

medium oil varnish   Varnish that contains 12–40 gallons of oil per 100 pounds of resin. Sometimes referred to as "all-purpose" varnish. It is not as durable as the long oil varnishes but it dries to a harder and glossier surface. It is more flexible than the short oil varnishes.

medullary rays   A specialized fluid channel found in some species of wood, most notably oak. The rays radiate from the center of the tree to the outside. In plain-sawed lumber the rays show up as short dashes dispersed uniformly over the surface. In quarter-sawed wood the rays make varied wild patterns. Quarter-sawed oak that has very prominent ray patterns is sometimes called "tiger oak" because the pattern resembles the stripes of a tiger.

meglip   A thickening agent used to improve the working characteristics of graining stains. The actual ingredients of the meglip vary depending on what type of stain it is added to. Traditional formulas used ingredients such as pumice, talc, whiting, cornstarch, varnish and stale beer.

mesh system   A system for gauging the size of abrasive particles. The particles are sorted through wire mesh screens. The higher the number the finer the abrasive. It is generally considered the most accurate system for designating the grade (coarseness) of coated abrasives.

methylene chloride   A nonflammable liquid (CH_3Cl) that dissolves most paints and many other finishes. It is frequently used in paint strippers and as a solvent in some finishing materials.

mildew   A fungus that feeds on oils found in paint and other finishing products. It causes discoloration of the paint.

mill marks   Marks left by a planer that give the surface of a board a wavy appearance.

mineral spirits   Petroleum-based solvents used in oil-based paints and varnishes. Paint thinner.

neoprene   A synthetic rubber that is especially resistant to chemicals and solvents. Recommended for use in protective gloves and clothing.

ngr stain   Non-grain-raising stain. An aniline dye stain that uses solvents other than water to dissolve the dye. It won't raise the grain as water stain does.

non-clog sandpaper   Sandpaper that has a special coating to keep material from sticking to the grit.

nylon   A synthetic plastic used to make brush filaments. Nylon brushes are particularly well suited for use with water-based materials.

oil colors   A pastelike combination of pigment and linseed oil or other oils. It is used to tint oil-based products. It should be thinned before mixing with the finish.

oiticica oil   An oil similar in characteristics to tung oil. It is derived from the Brazilian *Licania rigida* tree.

opaque   A substance that does not allow light to pass through it. In wood finishing, any finish that hides the underlying wood.

open-coat sandpaper   Sandpaper that has empty space surrounding each abrasive particle, as opposed to closed-coat which has the backing surface completely covered with grit. It doesn't cut as fast as closed-coat initially, but it will last longer when used on materials that tend to clog or gum up the sandpaper.

open-grain   The appearance of wood with large, visible pores that must be filled with paste filler to achieve a smooth surface. There are two types of open-grained wood: ring-porous and diffuse-porous. Ring-porous woods like oak and ash have large pores at the beginning of each annual ring. Diffuse-porous wood like Philippine mahogany (lauan) have large pores evenly distributed throughout the wood.

orange peel   An improperly sprayed surface with a texture that looks like the surface of an orange.

orange shellac   A refined grade of shellac that still retains some of the orangelike brown color of raw shellac.

overspray   Small droplets of the material being applied with a spray gun that miss the intended area and land on another surface.

ox hair   Hair obtained from the ears of cattle. It is used alone to make striping and sign painters' brushes or blended with China bristle to make high-quality brushes.

pad applicator   A finishing tool that consists of a foam pad covered with a piece of short-napped fabric. Originally designed for house painting, but it is well suited for other applications such as applying stain.

padding lacquer   A special type of lacquer formulated to be applied with a pad similar to the kind used when French polishing. Also called spot finishing lacquer, it is mostly used to repair damaged finishes. Unlike most lacquers, it can be applied directly over many finishes.

palmetto   A natural filament derived from the palmetto tree. It is sometimes used as a substitute for bristle in brushes.

paraffin oil   A mineral oil used as a lubricant for rubbing out a finish. Also called rubbing oil.

particle board   A man-made reconstituted wood product. It is made from very small wood chips or particles bonded together with glue under heat and pressure. There are several grades. The two most common grades are underlayment and industrial. Underlayment has a slightly rough surface and is intended for use under carpet or other flooring materials. Industrial grade particleboard has a very smooth surface and is denser than underlayment. It is intended for use in furniture and as a base for plastic laminates. Usually available in ½", ⅝" and ¾" thickness.

patina   The condition of a wood and its finish that develops over time. Usually it is characterized by a smooth, worn surface and darkening of the wood. Also includes the build-up of waxes and oils that have been applied to wood over time and the scars and marks that are acquired through use. Denotes a genuine antique.

penetrating oil stain   An oil-based stain that has oil-soluble dyes rather than pigments as an ingredient.

perilla oil   A natural oil derived from the seeds of the *Perilla ocymoides* plant. Its properties are somewhat between tung oil and linseed oil.

phenolic   A very durable synthetic resin made from phenol-formaldehyde and phenol-furfural. It is used to make finishing products that are resistant to water, chemicals and scratching.

pigmented oil stain   An oil-based stain that relies on pigments for its color. Also called wiping stain.

pigments   Minerals and chemicals selected for their color and ground to very fine particles.

plain-sawed   Wood that has been cut so that the annual rings make an angle of less than 45° with the surface of the board. Also called flat-grain or plain-sawn.

polyester brush filament   Filaments manufactured from polyester resin. Well suited for use with water-based finishes.

polyester resin   A synthetic resin. It is often used in two-part catalyzed finishes. It produces a tough, glossy film, but it is not as wear-resistant as epoxy.

polyethylene   A synthetic resin made by polymerizing ethylene. Since it is nontoxic and odorless it is used for food-related items. It is water-resistant and resists many chemicals.

polystyrene   A synthetic resin made from styrene. It is used in paints and varnishes.

polyurethane   One of the most widely used resins in synthetic varnish, it is also used in some paints. It can be chemically hardened by the addition of a catalyst. Oil-modified polyurethane air-dries. It produces a very durable finish that is resistant to wear and abrasion, water, and weathering. It is very resistant to chemicals and it retains its gloss longer than most finishes under hard wear.

pores   Small openings in the surface of a board. They result when the saw cuts open large, elongated cells (vessels) in the wood. The vessels serve as fluid channels in the living tree.

pressure-feed gun   A spray gun that is designed to use the pressure of compressed air to transfer liquid from the cup to the nozzle.

primary colors   Basic colors that can be mixed to form all other colors. For pigments the primary colors are red, blue, and yellow.

primer   A paint that is formulated to adhere well to bare wood and also bond to the next coat. It frequently incorporates a sealer that prevents bleed-through of stains from the wood.

proprietary solvent   *See* denatured alcohol.

psi   Pounds per square inch. A way to measure the pressure of compressed air.

pumice   A light volcanic glass that, in powdered form, is used for rubbing a finish. It is coarser than rottenstone.

putty   A pasty compound used to fill nail holes and defects in wood.

quarter-sawed   Wood that has been cut so that the annual rings form an angle of 45° to 90° with the surface. Also called edge-grain, vertical-grain, or quarter-sawn.

raised grain   A condition that occurs when water causes wood fibres to swell so that some stand above the surface of the board.

ray marker   A woodgraining tool used to imitate the dash-shaped marks made by medullary rays in plain-sawed oak. Consists of a number of small wheels that have short dashes embossed on their edges.

red sable   A natural brush filament obtained from Siberian mink and used for lettering or artists' brushes.

rejuvenator   Any of various products that are used to restore the appearance of an old finish.

resin   A synthetic or natural chemical that dries to a hard impervious film.

rotary-cut   Wood that is cut by rotating a log against a fixed knife to produce a continuous sheet. Most veneer and fir plywood is produced in this manner. Oak and birch plywood also frequently use rotary-cut veneers.

rottenstone   A natural abrasive made from powdered limestone. It is finer than pumice and is often used in a second step when rubbing out a finish.

rubbing compound   A commercially prepared mixture of abrasive powder and lubricant that is used for a final rubbing of a finished surface.

runs   A defect that occurs when too much finishing material is applied to a vertical surface.

safflower oil   A natural oil sometimes used in paint. It is derived from the safflower plant.

sandpaper   A coated abrasive with a paper backing. Originally the term applied only to flint paper, but now is applied to any type of abrasive paper.

sapwood   The *live* wood near the outside of a tree. Generally lighter in color and more prone to decay than heartwood which is in the center of a log.

satin   A term used to describe a finish that is not as dull as a flat finish, but does not have a high gloss.

sealer   A finishing material used to seal the pores of bare wood. Also, a coat used between two incompatible products or a type of primer that prevents bleeding.

shading stain   A lacquer-based product that contains dyes or pigments to color it. It is a semi-transparent surface coating that does not penetrate into the wood. Used extensively on mass-produced furniture.

shellac   A finishing material made from lac. Lac is a natural resin produced by small insects called *Laccifer lacca*. *See* button shellac, orange shellac, blond shellac, and white shellac.

short oil varnish   Varnish that contains 5–12 gallons of oil per 100 pounds of resin. The high percentage of resin makes the dry film very hard and glossy, but it is not as elastic or durable as varnish that contains more oil. Short oil varnishes are used when a rubbed finish is desired. Also called piano varnish, rubbing varnish, or polishing varnish.

silex filler (paste filler)   A product made by mixing boiled linseed oil with powdered silex and driers. Used to fill the pores of open-grained wood. Usually comes as a paste that must be thinned before use. Silex is a natural mineral. It is a form of silica derived from quartz.

silicon carbide   One of the hardest synthetic abrasives used for wood finishing. It is produced in an electric furnace by combining silicon and carbon. Its chemical formula is SiC. Its most common use in wood finishing is in wet-or-dry sandpaper.

softwood   Wood produced by trees that have needles rather than broad leaves. The term has no relation to the actual hardness of the wood.

solvent   A liquid used to dissolve other substances. Sometimes it also refers to a liquid used to hold small particles such as pigments in suspension without actually dissolving them. The solvents of finishing products usually evaporate leaving only the other ingredients to form the final film. Popular solvents for wood finishing products are: turpentine, mineral spirits, naphtha, benzine, alcohol, acetone, methyl ethyl ketone, and toluene. While it is usually not thought of as such, water is actually a solvent.

soybean oil   Also called soya oil. It has properties similar to linseed oil and is often used in paint.

spirit stain   A wood stain that uses alcohol for its solvent.

spiriting off   The final step in French polishing. A clean pad dampened with alcohol is used to remove the lubricating oil from the finished surface.

spontaneous combustion   Self-ignition resulting from chemical reaction. When oily rags are piled together and there is no air circulation the oxidizing oils will generate enough heat to cause the rags to burn without any external ignition source.

stain   Any of several products used to artificially color wood. Stains may have dyes, pigments or chemicals that produce the color. Stains may either penetrate into the wood, form a film on the surface or react chemically with substances in the wood.

stripper   Any product that uses chemicals or solvents to soften an old finish for removal. Paint stripper.

sunflower oil   A natural oil with properties similar to linseed oil.

sword striper   A brush with very long flexible filaments that is used for pin-striping and freehand graining.

synthetic varnish   Varnish that uses man-made resins in place of natural resins.

syphon-feed gun   A spray gun that uses atmospheric pressure to deliver liquid from the cup to the nozzle.

tack rag   A piece of cheesecloth that has been treated so that it attracts dust.

tampico   A natural filament derived from plants in the cactus family. It is resistant to chemicals and is used primarily in brushes used to apply chemical stains.

tannin   An acid found in wood. It forms different-colored compounds when it reacts with certain chemicals. Most chemical stains depend on a reaction with the tannin in wood.

tinting colors   Pigments suspended in any of several liquids. They are used to tint or color finishing products.

tung oil   A natural oil derived from the seeds of the Chinese tung tree. It is used by itself or mixed with other oils to make penetrating oil finishes. It is also used in many paints and varnishes. It dries faster and harder than linseed oil. Also called China wood oil, China nut oil, or nut oil. It is manufactured in South America.

turning   A piece of wood that has been shaped on a lathe.

turpentine   A solvent used in oil-based finishes. It is distilled from the gum of pine trees. Because it is more expensive than other solvents like mineral spirits, turpentine is not included in most modern formulas. It is still regarded as the ideal thinner for products containing linseed oil because it increases brushability and flowing characteristics and because it aids in the drying process by conveying oxygen to the oil.

universal tinting colors   Tinting colors that are compatible with oil- or water-based products. Their liquid consistency makes them easier to mix than the paste-type tinting colors. Even though they are called universal, they may not be compatible with some lacquers, epoxies, or catalyzed finishes. Check for compatibility before using with these products.

value   The lightness or darkness of a color. Adding white lightens a color's value, while adding black darkens its value.

varnish   A transparent finish made with natural or synthetic resins and oils. They harden by combining with oxygen and are more resistant to water and alcohol than shellac.

varnish stain   A colored varnish that stains and varnishes the surface in one step.

vegetable stain   Stain that derives its color from natural plant dyes instead of chemical dyes or pigments.

vehicle   The liquid part of a finish. It consists of the solvents, oils, and resins.

veneer   A thin (¼″ or less) sheet of wood. Face veneers are usually made from expensive wood species and applied over cheaper woods. Core veneers are made from inexpensive woods like fir and are used for the inner plies in plywood. Veneers may be produced by rotary process, slicing or sawing.

vertical-grain lumber   Another name for quarter-sawed lumber.

vinyl   A general name for several synthetic resins including polyvinyl acetate, polyvinyl chloride, and polyvinyl butyral. The dry film of most vinyls is colorless, tasteless, odorless, nontoxic, abrasion resistant, chemical resistant, weather resistant and flexible.

water-emulsion varnish   Commonly called latex varnish. It is a water-based product that produces a varnishlike finish. The resins are emulsified in water much like they are in latex paint.

water stain   A clear, permanent aniline dye stain that uses water as its solvent. It will raise the grain of the wood because it uses water.

wax   A fatty substance that may be animal, vegetable, or mineral in its origin. Beeswax is obtained from honeycombs. Paraffin wax is a petroleum product. Carnauba wax is from the Brazilian wax palm, and ceresin is a synthetic wax. Wax is used to polish and protect a finish. Some antique finishes use wax as the only protective coat.

wet-or-dry sandpaper   Sandpaper that uses waterproof glue to attach the abrasive particles to a water-resistant paper backing.

white shellac   The most highly refined grade of shellac. It is bleached to remove all of the orange cast of the raw shellac.

whitewood   Wood that has not yet been finished. Even if the natural color of the wood is quite dark it is called whitewood in this respect.

wood putty   A doughy product used to fill nail holes and defects in wood.

wrinkles   A finishing defect that occurs when the underlying finish dries more slowly than the top surface. This causes the top surface to have a wrinkled texture.

INDEX

WEIGHTS AND MEASURES

Unit	Abbreviation	Equivalents In Other Units of Same System	Metric Equivalent
Weight			
Avoirdupois			
ton			
short ton		20 short hundredweight, 2000 pounds	0.907 metric tons
long ton		20 long hundredweight, 2240 pounds	1.016 metric tons
hundredweight	cwt		
short hundredweight		100 pounds, 0.05 short tons	45.359 kilograms
long hundredweight		112 pounds, 0.05 long tons	50.802 kilograms
pound	lb *or* lb av *also* #	16 ounces, 7000 grains	0.453 kilograms
ounce	oz *or* oz av	16 drams, 437.5 grains	28.349 grams
dram	dr *or* dr av	27.343 grains, 0.0625 ounces	1.771 grams
grain	gr	0.036 drams, 0.002285 ounces	0.0648 grams
Troy			
pound	lb t	12 ounces, 240 pennyweight, 5760 grains	0.373 kilograms
ounce	oz t	20 pennyweight, 480 grains	31.103 grams
pennyweight	dwt *also* pwt	24 grains, 0.05 ounces	1.555 grams
grain	gr	0.042 pennyweight, 0.002083 ounces	0.0648 grams
Apothecaries'			
pound	lb ap	12 ounces, 5760 grains	0.373 kilograms
ounce	oz ap	8 drams, 480 grains	31.103 grams
dram	dr ap	3 scruples, 60 grains	3.887 grams
scruple	s ap	20 grains, 0.333 drams	1.295 grams
grain	gr	0.05 scruples, 0.002083 ounces, 0.0166 drams	0.0648 grams
Capacity			
U.S. Liquid Measure			
gallon	gal	4 quarts (2.31 cubic inches)	3.785 litres
quart	qt	2 pints (57.75 cubic inches)	0.946 litres
pint	pt	4 gills (28.875 cubic inches)	0.473 litres
gill	gi	4 fluidounces (7.218 cubic inches)	118.291 millilitres
fluidounce	fl oz	8 fluidrams (1.804 cubic inches)	29.573 millilitres
fluidram	fl dr	60 minims (0.225 cubic inches)	3.696 millilitres
minim	min	1/60 fluidram (0.003759 cubic inches)	0.061610 millilitres
U.S. Dry Measure			
bushel	bu	4 pecks (2150.42 cubic inches)	35.238 litres
peck	pk	8 quarts (537.605 cubic inches)	8.809 litres
quart	qt	2 pints (67.200 cubic inches)	1.101 litres
pint	pt	½ quart (33.600 cubic inches)	0.550 litres
British Imperial Liquid and Dry Measure			
bushel	bu	4 pecks (2219.36 cubic inches)	0.036 cubic metres
peck	pk	2 gallons (554.84 cubic inches)	0.009 cubic metres
gallon	gal	4 quarts (277.420 cubic inches)	4.545 litres
quart	qt	2 pints (69.355 cubic inches)	1.136 litres
pint	pt	4 gills (34.678 cubic inches)	568.26 cubic centimetres
gill	gi	5 fluidounces (8.669 cubic inches)	142.066 cubic centimetres
fluidounce	fl oz	8 fluidrams (1.7339 cubic inches)	28.416 cubic centimetres
fluidram	fl dr	60 minims (0.216734 cubic inches)	3.5516 cubic centimetres
minim	min	1/60 fluidram (0.003612 cubic inches)	0.059194 cubic centimetres
Length			
mile	mi	5280 feet, 320 rods, 1760 yards	1.609 kilometres
rod	rd	5.50 yards, 16.5 feet	5.029 metres
yard	yd	3 feet, 36 inches	0.914 metres
foot	ft *or* '	12 inches, 0.333 yards	30.480 centimetres
inch	in *or* "	0.083 feet, 0.027 yards	2.540 centimetres
Area			
square mile	sq mi *or* m²	640 acres, 102,400 square rods	2.590 square kilometres
acre		4840 square yards, 43,560 square feet	0.405 hectares, 4047 square metres
square rod	sq rd *or* rd²	30.25 square yards, 0.006 acres	25.293 square metres
square yard	sq yd *or* yd²	1296 square inches, 9 square feet	0.836 square metres
square foot	sq ft *or* ft²	144 square inches, 0.111 square yards	0.093 square metres
square inch	sq in *or* in²	0.007 square feet, 0.00077 square yards	6.451 square centimetres

METRIC SYSTEM

Unit	Abbreviation				Approximate U.S. Equivalent

Length

Unit	Abbreviation	Number of Metres	Approximate U.S. Equivalent
myriametre	mym	10,000	6.2 miles
kilometre	km	1000	0.62 mile
hectometre	hm	100	109.36 yards
dekametre	dam	10	32.81 feet
metre	m	1	39.37 inches
decimetre	dm	0.1	3.94 inches
centimetre	cm	0.01	0.39 inch
millimetre	mm	0.001	0.04 inch

Area

Unit	Abbreviation	Number of Square Metres	Approximate U.S. Equivalent
square kilometre	sq km or km²	1,000,000	0.3861 square miles
hectare	ha	10,000	2.47 acres
are	a	100	119.60 square yards
centare	ca	1	10.76 square feet
square centimetre	sq cm or cm²	0.0001	0.155 square inch

Volume

Unit	Abbreviation	Number of Cubic Metres	Approximate U.S. Equivalent
dekastere	das	10	13.10 cubic yards
stere	s	1	1.31 cubic yards
decistere	ds	0.10	3.53 cubic feet
cubic centimetre	cu cm or cm³ also cc	0.000001	0.061 cubic inch

Capacity

Unit	Abbreviation	Number of Litres	Cubic	Dry	Liquid
kilolitre	kl	1000	1.31 cubic yards		
hectolitre	hl	100	3.53 cubic feet	2.84 bushels	
dekalitre	dal	10	0.35 cubic foot	1.14 pecks	2.64 gallons
litre	l	1	61.02 cubic inches	0.908 quart	1.057 quarts
decilitre	dl	0.10	6.1 cubic inches	0.18 pint	0.21 pint
centilitre	cl	0.01	0.6 cubic inch		0.338 fluidounce
millilitre	ml	0.001	0.06 cubic inch		0.27 fluidram

Mass and Weight

Unit	Abbreviation	Number of Grams	Approximate U.S. Equivalent
metric ton	MT or t	1,000,000	1.1 tons
quintal	q	100,000	220.46 pounds
kilogram	kg	1,000	2.2046 pounds
hectogram	hg	100	3.527 ounces
dekagram	dag	10	0.353 ounce
gram	g or gm	1	0.035 ounce
decigram	dg	0.10	1.543 grains
centigram	cg	0.01	0.154 grain
milligram	mg	0.001	0.015 grain

ABOUT THE AUTHOR

Sam Allen began woodworking at age twelve when he received a Swiss Army knife for Christmas and decided to use it to carve a chess set. By age fifteen he was adding a room to his house and restoring an antique Model "T" Ford (which unlike modern cars contained a lot of wood). In high school he used every loophole he could find in the rules to add more shop classes to his schedule until he was in shop classes for five of the seven class periods in his senior year.

He began experiments with new finishing techniques and little used traditional methods at Brigham Young University, College of Industrial and Technical Education, where he was studying woodworking. These experiments continued after college while he worked as a carpenter and cabinetmaker.

His experiments with wood graining grew out of his interest in historic buildings in his native Utah. Many old buildings in Utah contain beautiful examples of classic wood graining, because the local mountains had no hardwood trees when the first settlers arrived. They used the native red pine for most of their woodwork, but they painted it to look like all of the hardwoods they left behind in the East.

Mr. Allen is a widely published free-lance author. He has had articles in *Popular Mechanics*, *The Woodworker's Journal*, *Fine Woodworking*, *Handy Andy*, and *Pacific Woodworker*.